THE
WILDLIFE GARDEN
month-by-month

THE
WILDLIFE GARDEN
month-by-month

JACKIE BENNETT

Photographs by Richard Hanson

David & Charles

A DAVID & CHARLES BOOK

Copyright © Jackie Bennett, 1993
First published 1993
Reprinted 1994, 1995
First paperback edition 1997

A catalogue record for this book is available from the British
Library.

ISBN 0 7153 0033 4 hardback
ISBN 0 7153 0573 5 paperback

Illustrations by Avis Murray
Book design by Diana Knapp

Typeset by ABM Typographics Ltd, Hull
and printed in Glasgow
by Bath Colour Books
for David & Charles
Brunel House Newton Abbot Devon

CONTENTS

INTRODUCTION

In the context of garden history as a whole, wildlife gardening is a relative newcomer. Like many new ideas, it has taken some time to become accepted by the gardening establishment and for its practitioners not to be considered as dangerous 'alternatives'. My first brush with the idea of inviting wildlife *into* the garden (rather than trying to keep it out) was in the early 1980s, when I was helping to plan the opening of a new theatre complex in the city of Stoke-on-Trent. The theatre grounds were being converted into an urban nature reserve with ponds, meadows and woodland, providing a much-needed resource for local schoolchildren and theatregoers.

Designed by landscape consultant Chris Baines, it was an incredibly brave and innovative concept at the time – and one which must have risked considerable professional ridicule. The essence of the plan was contained on just four sheets of paper with the headings: Meadow, Woodland Edge,

Hedgerow and Water – not the usual terminology of architects who generally talk only of 'hard landscaping' and 'stone-effect paving'. It was nevertheless a very simple but effective way of mentally dividing up a plot of land, be it a domestic garden or a potential building site.

Those four sheets of paper have travelled with me ever since. The basic good sense of the idea of creating landscapes for wildlife, as well as for people, had converted me to wildlife gardening long before I ever had a garden. Nowadays, wildlife gardening is quite a respectable activity and we can all play a part in the revolution that Chris Baines and the conservationists started. But, as with all revolutions, we need a handbook in order to make those ideas work in our own particular situation. This book is therefore first and foremost a practical *gardening* book – for all those people who are swept away by the spirit of wildlife gardening, but have never quite got round to converting that enthusiasm into reality.

SEASONS AND MONTHS

Under average conditions, the terms 'early', 'mid' and 'late' season as used throughout the book correspond to the following months:

SPRING
Early: March
Mid: April
Late: May

SUMMER
Early: June
Mid: July
Late: August

AUTUMN
Early: September
Mid: October
Late: November

WINTER
Early: December
Mid: January
Late: February

(opposite) *In autumn, the fallen leaves of deciduous trees carpet the woodland floor and create an extra wildlife resource*

Red campion (Silene dioica) makes a colourful component of the summer-flowering meadow. In the wild, it may hybridise naturally with the white campion to produce an even paler pink

PLANT TYPES

Plants are described by their commonly used names (where applicable) as well as by their botanical name. Plants should be considered hardy unless stated otherwise.

ANNUAL
Germinates and flowers the same year, then dies.

BIENNIAL
Germinates one year, flowers the next, then dies.

PERENNIAL
Survives for many years.

BULB
Underground storage organ, developed from bases of the leaves.

CORM
Underground storage organ, developed from the bases of the stems.

RHIZOME
Underground stem.

TUBER
Underground organ, developed from the roots and underground stems.

SHRUB
Woody plant, branching from ground level, usually smaller than a tree.

TREE
Woody plant with a central trunk, usually taller growing than a shrub.

BACK TO BASICS

The secret of making a haven for wildlife, on whatever scale, is to recreate the habitats found in nature. To the four headings above (water, woodland edge, meadow and hedgerow) I would add wetland, flower borders, compost heap and, most importantly, an untidy patch which is barely 'gardened' at all.

Most gardeners already have some of these habitats although they might not think of them in those terms. Gardening for wildlife does not necessarily mean changing the structure of the garden or throwing out the received wisdom of conventional gardening. There are, however, some key issues to be considered. Chemicals and wildlife, for example, are not, on the whole, complementary. There are of course some chemical products available which do not leave a residue in the soil and there are those which are designed to be more selective in the pests that they kill. Everyone has his/her own level of tolerance, of how many leaf holes he can accept, before reaching for the spray. Bear in mind however that every input of chemical, natural-based or artificially manufactured, upsets the balance of pest and pest-eater. Many scientists believe that aphids manage to produce exactly the right number of offspring to support the current population of ladybirds. By wiping out one, we deprive the other of its main means of survival. One of the major arguments for not trying to control pests, is that birds and insects, if left alone, do it so much more effectively.

The most liberating aspect of wildlife gardening is knowing that a little untidiness is a good thing. Suddenly the pressure to keep up appearances is gone and it is socially acceptable to sweep the leaves under the hedge and leave piles of clippings in a corner. Having said that, wildlife gardens do have to be managed.

Native plants are the first choice, not because of some purist philosophy, but because, in general, they support a greater range of species. Nevertheless, birds, insects and mammals are great opportunists and, having established essential ecological relationships with native trees, shrubs and meadow flowers, they will top up their food supplies from any nectar- or berry-bearing import.

In this book, non-native plants are included if they are particularly useful to wildlife; by the same token native plants, and especially endangered species which gardeners can help to conserve, are included and considered to be 'wildlife'. Strictly speaking, 'native' plants – those which were present in the British Isles before the rise in sea-levels finally separated the islands from the continent of Europe – are a fairly limited group, and since many more species have become 'naturalised' than are truly native, the two are generally grouped together. Naturalised plants may have been imported (accidentally or otherwise) but they behave like natives, thriving in the prevailing climate and soils without human intervention. When we think about creating a wild garden (as opposed to a wildlife garden) we should think only of these native and naturalised plants that take care of themselves. Gardening for wildlife, on the other hand, allows the gardener to draw on a much wider range of plant species, be they native, naturalised or exotic.

One important facet of gardening for wildlife that is sometimes overlooked is the use of colour. Most gardeners employ some element of design in choosing plants in colours that they like or that blend in with an overall colour scheme. For wildlife, and

insects in particular, we might make different choices. Flowers may be pollinated by wind and other methods but mainly they rely on insects. The colours and patterns of flowers are not primarily for our benefit, but function as a signalling system to attract these insects: butterflies and flies like yellows and blues, bees prefer blues, reds and purples (which reflect ultraviolet light) and moths go to white. Scent works in co-operation with colour; butterflies seem to gravitate towards heavy scents and bees to lighter, sweeter ones. Moths being night-flying are attracted to those plants which are at their most fragrant in the evening, such as honeysuckle and white campion.

As gardeners, we can be choosy about who (or what) we invite into our gardens. People who live on the edge of a deer forest know how quickly a young rose bush can be stripped of its leaves by roaming deer. Others, living in cities, would gladly sacrifice their roses for even the most fleeting glimpse of a mammal of this size. Similar arguments apply to foxes and squirrels. We cannot control nature, but we can to some extent welcome or discourage certain sections of the wildlife population. Conventional gardening books are full of tips to frighten away unwanted wildlife and it is these that the reader must turn to if certain species have become a nuisance. This book starts from the premise that the reader wants to attract a greater range of creatures into the garden.

USING THE BOOK

By dividing the book into months, the aim is to make practical information accessible to the gardener at any time of the year. If, for example, you would like to know which routine jobs should be undertaken in the wildlife garden at a particular time of year,

simply turn to the 'Tasks for the Month' pages for that month. On the other hand, if you want to locate information on specific plants, habitats, creatures and so on, use the index to direct you to the appropriate pages.

Each chapter is divided into four sections: an introduction to the wildlife and weather to be expected that month, a checklist of the main tasks and instructions on how to carry them out, profiles of plants which are useful to wildlife, and a major practical project for those who want to increase the range of habitats available to wildlife. (For those wanting to find out about different habitats and their value in the garden, the practical project section also provides an overview.) In addition, the Appendices provide information on wildlife gardening with containers, as well as a selection of garden plans, which can be used as a starting point for your own ideas.

In some areas, the seasons may not coincide exactly with those of the book. For this reason, the terms mid-spring and late autumn are used to denote planting and sowing times, for example, rather than specify a month which might be incorrect for particularly cold or mild regions. With experience, gardeners get to know the vagaries of their own climate; but the table on page 7 may be used as a guide for average conditions.

Too many of us worry about the state of our gardens, thinking of them as an extension of the house to be cleaned up and made tidy. I hope this book will help more people actually *enjoy* their gardens and let the local wildlife judge whether or not they come up to standard.

KEY TO PLANT LISTS

Throughout the book you will find lists of plants for specific uses. These have been coded as follows:

B   = Bee plant
C   = Caterpillar food plant
N   = Butterfly nectar plant
S   = Seeds for birds
F   = Fruit/berries/nuts for birds/
        mammals
H   = Attractive to hoverflies
I   = Large number of
        associated insects
Nat = Native or naturalised
        species
Po = Poisonous
E   = Evergreen
M   = Moths
R   = Rare in the wild
W   = Suitable for wetland garden

9

JANUARY

One of the best things about a wildlife garden is that winter is a season to be welcomed rather than dreaded. Unlike a conventional garden, where a small selection of carefully chosen shrubs provides artificial 'winter colour', the wildlife garden is rich in its own seasonal plants, birds and animals. Gardeners tend to dislike this time of year, yet this feeling that everything is 'on hold' is part of its charm. If a layer of snow falls, there is little to beat the absolute stillness of a winter's day. Of course, this calm is deceptive and lasts only as long as it takes for the first track marks to appear in the virgin snow. Just beneath the surface, the garden is teeming with life.

Keeping an eye on the bird table from the warmth of the kitchen or living-room is one of the month's chief pleasures. A great cross-section of users should show up, including all the regulars like blackbirds, thrushes, tits and robins. There may also be flocks of migrant fieldfares, redwing or siskins seeking shelter in suburbia from the cutting winds of the open fields.

When the temperature does lift above freezing and the sun emerges temporarily to warm the earth, creatures like hedgehogs, which are normally hibernating, may stir from under a pile of leaves at the bottom of the hedge for a short food foray. Foxes are often seen in gardens during a hard winter, foraging for slugs and beetles. They are not averse to turning over a few rubbish bins either in their search for food.

As for plants, the snowdrop has become something of a cliché for the new year. Yet the timing of the flower is perfect; just as we have given up hope of seeing a living plant, it emerges through the melting snow – a constant reminder that this is anything but the dead of winter.

tasks

FOR THE

month

DISCOURAGE SCAVENGERS
Do not leave uneaten bird food out
overnight as it can attract rats and
mice.

CHECKLIST

- Start a wildlife notebook
- Feed birds consistently
- Keep pond free of ice
- Draw up plans for a wildlife garden
- Order wildflower seeds

STARTING A WILDLIFE NOTEBOOK

At the start of the year, make a resolution to record the activity in your garden for one whole twelve-month cycle. Use a hardbacked notebook or desk diary and keep it somewhere near at hand so you can make notes when you come in from the garden. Every event is worth recording, from the appearance of the first snowdrop to the last holly berry disappearing in the beak of a visiting fieldfare.

Keeping a notebook is not just a pleasant exercise, it will also help you to plan next year's garden and monitor changes in the frequency and behaviour of local wildlife. It doesn't need to be elaborate or a literary masterpiece, just the date and a few notes will do. As the garden develops and the range of species increases, it will provide a lasting record not only for your own use, but perhaps for future owners of your house and garden.

LOOKING AFTER THE BIRDS

This is probably the month during which garden birds benefit most from a little human intervention.

Natural food sources like windfallen apples and hawthorn berries have been used up by the population of local birds, in competition with visitors from the Arctic north who take refuge in gardens at this time of year. Insects are in hibernation, the ground is frozen solid and water sources are iced over. It is therefore vital to feed birds regularly, putting out food every day. Early morning is the best time, although you can put out a second 'feed' in the early afternoon. Fresh water is important too, even if you have a pond – many birds will drink from the bird table and wash their feathers in the pond.

Put out a range of food, on the ground and on the table (see p132-3 on choosing a bird table). Include hanging feeders with nuts for tits, sparrows and rarer visitors like siskins; apples on the ground for blackbirds and thrushes; and seeds, nuts and fat on the table for robins, starlings and other species. They will come to rely on this food supply, so once you've begun to feed keep it up until the worst of the winter is over.

Recommended Bird Food

- *Peanuts* These should be unsalted, although the salt can be washed off and the nuts dried thoroughly. Commercially produced nuts should bear the Birdfood Standards Association's seal of approval. This guarantees the nuts are free from contamination by aflatoxin, a toxin produced in nuts which have not been harvested and packed correctly, sometimes resulting in death to birds who eat them.
- *Sunflower seeds* Wild bird food mixtures containing sunflower and other seeds are available from suppliers advertising in bird magazines and, increasingly, from hardware and pet shops.
- *Half a coconut* Drill a hole in the top and use string to hang the shell downwards so that it stays dry. Don't use desiccated

RECIPE for bird cake

¹/₄kg (¹/₂lb) suet or lard, melted

¹/₂kg (1lb) dry 'cake' mixture: seeds, nuts, oats, dried fruit, cake etc

A mould: small bowl, half a coconut shell or empty plastic carton

Put the dry mixture into the mould and pour the melted fat over it. If you intend to hang the 'cake' from the bird table, place a piece of string in the bowl before pouring in the fat. Leave to set and tip out the cake onto the bird table.

coconut as it tends to swell up inside the bird.

■ *Kitchen scraps* Not all food scraps are suitable. Try bacon rind, suet, dry porridge oats, cheese, baked potatoes, apples and raisins. Stale bread or cake is acceptable but it should be soaked in water to make it easier to swallow.

KEEPING THE POND ICE FREE

It is important to keep at least some part of the pond free of ice throughout any cold spells. This not only allows birds and other visitors like foxes to drink but also stops a build-up of gases under the ice. As organic matter decomposes gases are released which, if trapped by a layer of ice, will build up and poison existing pond life. A simple and cheap method of allowing the pond to 'breathe' is to float a block of wood on the surface of the water. Then, when the pond freezes remove the wood, leaving a gap. A child's plastic or foam ball will also prevent ice forming over all the surface, but avoid lurid colours which can scare away potential users.

MAKING PLANS

This is the best month for planning out a new garden layout (see Appendix 2 for suggested plans). Even if you only envisage a few minor changes, it is a good idea to try them out on paper beforehand. If you are starting with a bare plot or considering a fairly major project like digging a pond or planting a mini-

woodland, it is essential to think it through in some detail before you ever put spade to earth.

Habitat/Feature
CHECKLIST

- [ ] Pond
- [ ] Marsh/bog area
- [ ] Mature living trees
- [ ] Old hollow/fallen trees
- [ ] Young trees
- [ ] Climbing plants
- [ ] Native mixed hedge
- [ ] Compost heap/bin
- [ ] Bird table
- [ ] Bird/bat boxes
- [ ] Berry-bearing shrubs
- [ ] Nectar-rich flowers
- [ ] Untidy corner
- [ ] Long grass/meadow area

Consider first of all which features already in the garden are useful to wildlife – mature trees, for instance, a compost heap or a pond of some kind. Use the list above to identify elements you want to keep. Draw a rough plan of the garden and mark in these features. Next, decide which features could be improved to make them more wildlife friendly, such as adding stepping stones to a steep-sided pond or replanting an existing border with nectar-rich flowers. You might wish to turn part of the lawn over to a wildflower meadow but, before you do, consider which areas it would be practical to grow long and which parts you really need to keep as a

conventional lawn. Be prepared to play around with this plan – all winter if you have to. Try all sorts of combinations, bearing in mind how much work they will involve, until you are happy that the layout is one that will suit you and your lifestyle, as well as the needs of the wildlife you want to attract.

ORDERING WILDFLOWER SEEDS

Many native species are not yet available as pot-grown plants in garden centres. This means that there is no option but to grow some varieties from seed which is more readily available. You will need to order from one of the wildflower specialists (listed on p140), or check out the seed packet displays in supermarkets and garden centres.

Annual flowers are particularly easy to grow and they don't necessarily have to be native as long as they are colourful and nectar-rich. Night-scented stocks, cornflowers, candytuft, snapdragons and sunflowers will attract insects and therefore increase the range of birds that visit the garden. Half-hardy annuals and biennial plants can also be raised from seed and incorporated in borders, where they will act as a magnet to summer bees and butterflies. (See pages 29, 40 and 65 for sowing details.)

If space is a problem, hardy and half-hardy annual seeds can be sown directly into large pots, where they can be left to grow on to full size. The pots can then be moved around the patio to create instant colour.

FLOWER SEEDS
HALF-HARDY ANNUALS
African marigold
(Tagetes erecta) N, B
French marigold
(Tagetes patula) N, B
Heliotrope *(Heliotropium)* N
Petunia N
Tobacco plant *(Nicotiana)* N
HARDY ANNUALS
Candytuft *(Iberis umbellata)* N
Common poppy
(Papaver rhoeas) B, H, Nat
Corncockle
(Agrostemma githago) N, Po, Nat
Corn chamomile
(Anthemis arvensis) N, Nat
Cornflower
(Centaurea cyanus) N, B, Nat
Larkspur
(Delphinium consolida) B, Po, Nat
Love-in-a-mist
(Nigella damascena) N
Mignonette
(Reseda odorata) N, C
Nasturtium
(Tropaeolum majus) H, C
Night-scented stock
(Matthiola bicornis) N, M
Poached egg flower
(Limnanthes douglasii) B, H
Pot marigold
(Calendula officinalis) B, H
Sunflower
(Helianthus annuus) N, B, S
Virginia stock
(Malcolmia maritima) N, B
BIENNIALS
Evening primrose
(Oenothera biennis) B, H, M
Forget-me-not
(Myosotis sylvatica) N, B, Nat
Foxglove
(Digitalis purpurea) B, Po, Nat
Great mullein
(Verbascum thapsus) B, Nat
Sweet rocket
(Hesperis matronalis) N, Nat
Sweet William
(Dianthus barbatus) N
Teasel
(Dipsacus fullonum) N, B, S, Nat
Wallflower
(Cheiranthus cheiri) N, Nat

plants
OF THE
month

▼ COMMON SNOWDROP
(Galanthus nivalis)

The common snowdrop, found widely in damp woodlands, on banks and in hedgerows, provides the first flowers of the year. A pretty plant which looks best planted in natural 'drifts'.

type	Bulb
flowers	White, inner petals tipped with green
height	13–20cm (5–8in), mid-winter to early spring
planting	Plant bulbs in early autumn, 5cm (2in) deep and 8cm (3in) apart
site	Partly shaded. In grass, under trees, shrubs or hedges
soil	Any, but grows best in rich, moist soils
care	May take two to three years to get established but needs no attention
propagation	When the clumps outgrow their space, lift and divide the bulbs immediately after flowering
varieties	'S. Arnott' is a larger, sweetly scented hybrid and 'Viridapicis' has green markings on the outer as well as inner petals
wildlife value	The scent acts as a signal to insects waking up prematurely from hibernation. On warm days, when there are more likely to be insects about, the petals open to their fullest

▲ HONEYSUCKLE
(Lonicera fragrantissima)

The winter-flowering honeysuckle is not native to Britain (unlike the wild honeysuckle or woodbine, *L. periclymenum*) but it is well worth growing for its fragrant flowers and foliage cover.

type	Partly evergreen climbing shrub
flowers	Creamy white, early winter to early spring
height	1.8m (6ft)
planting	Plant in mid- to late spring, against walls, fences or trellis, or in containers
site	Sun or light shade – ideally the roots should be in shade and the top in sun
soil	Any well-drained soil
care	Mulch around the plant with leaf mould or compost in spring. Regular pruning is not necessary, but straggly or overgrown plants should have old wood removed after flowering
propagation	Stem cuttings in mid- to late summer
related species	*L. standishii* is similar but grows to a more compact 1.2m (4ft)
wildlife value	The foliage may provide cover for birds and the flowers are welcoming to insects when the rest of the garden is bare

COMMON SNOWDROP

VIBURNUM

(Viburnum x *bodnantense)*

Not a native shrub, but a very hardy species bearing clusters of flowers on bare wood even in the hardest winter.

type	Deciduous shrub
flowers	White flushed with pink, throughout winter
height	3m (10ft)
spread	2.75m (9ft)
planting	Plant from mid-autumn to early spring, adding some garden compost or well-rotted manure to the planting hole
site	Full sun or light shade
soil	Moist, fertile
care	No regular pruning needed, but if the shrub becomes overgrown, thin out in mid-spring
propagation	From cuttings in late summer to early autumn
wildlife value	Flowering shrubs are few and far between this month and the blooms of *Viburnum bodnantense* have a particularly good perfume to attract insects

WINTER ACONITE

WINTER ACONITE

(Eranthis hyemalis)

Originally an introduction from Europe and Asia, this member of the buttercup family is naturalised in many parts of Britain and widely grown in gardens. The dazzling yellow flowers appear before or at the same time as snow-drops.

type	Tuber
flowers	Bright yellow, mid-winter to early spring
height	10cm (4in)
planting	Plant tubers in late summer, 3–5cm (1–2in) deep and 8cm (3in) apart in groups of six or more
site	Sun whilst flowering, partial shade for the rest of the year. Under deciduous trees or between shrubs
soil	Moist, humus-rich, leaf mould
care	No special care
propagation	Plants will naturally set seed and spread. Alternatively, lift and divide tubers immediately after flowering
wildlife value	Provides early pollen for waking insects. The winter aconite relies on flies and bees for pollination

practical project

MAKING A BAT BOX

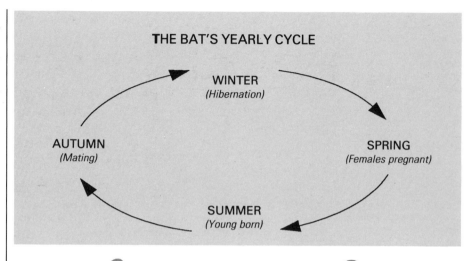

THE BAT'S YEARLY CYCLE

WINTER *(Hibernation)*

SPRING *(Females pregnant)*

SUMMER *(Young born)*

AUTUMN *(Mating)*

WHY ENCOURAGE BATS?

Many species of bats are becoming rare and in some cases nearing extinction because of disturbance and loss of natural roost sites. In cities and intensively farmed areas, their food supply of insects is also becoming depleted. A healthy garden with a wide range of insects will provide a rich night-time hunting ground. By eating a large proportion of pests like midges, the bats will help to maintain the garden's natural balance.

By understanding bats' natural cycle we can choose the best ways to encourage them to use our gardens and houses. Bats traditionally roost in hollow trees or in caves, but have increasingly become adapted to buildings. For winter hibernation they will seek out a well-insulated spot with a constant temperature, such as a cave or cellar, but it is quite difficult to provide these conditions artificially. During the rest of the year, bats are less particular and will use a number of different sites. In spring they will seek out a safe place to give birth and rear their young. In summer they may choose a cooler spot to roost and in autumn a slightly warmer one. If your garden has any old trees they may well be inhabited by bats. If not, it is even more important to put up bat boxes.

SITING THE BOX

Position bat boxes at 3–5m (10–15ft) above ground (or higher), on a tree, post or on the house wall. Make sure the bats have a clear flight path by removing overhanging branches or other obstructions. If possible, site three boxes facing north, south-west and south-east. This will enable bats to select the most suitable roost for the time of year.

CONSTRUCTING THE BOX

A bat box works on the same principle as a bird box, except that instead of a hole at the front there is a gap underneath. The roof is removable.

■ Use a rough-sawn plank of untreated softwood, 2.5cm (1in) thick, 15cm (6in) wide and 1.2m (4ft) long. (If the wood is too smooth, you will need to roughen it with saw cuts to enable the bats to cling properly.)

■ Mark up the plank as shown and cut out the pieces for the front, back, two sides, roof and base of the box.

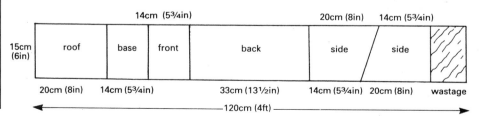

	14cm (5¾in)				20cm (8in)	14cm (5¾in)	
15cm (6in)	roof	base	front	back	side	side	
	20cm (8in)	14cm (5¾in)		33cm (13½in)	14cm (5¾in)	20cm (8in)	wastage

←————————————— 120cm (4ft) —————————————→

■ Taking the back plate, drill holes at the top and bottom to take the nails or screws needed to fix it to the tree. Also, cut a groove 6mm (¼in) deep and 2.5cm (1in) wide, 5cm (2in) from the top of the back plate – this is for the roof piece to slot into.

groove

■ Taking the roof section, nail a wooden batten to the underside, 3.5cm (1½in) from the front. The wooden batten should be 12 × 3 × 2cm (5 × 1¼ × ¾in). This will stop the roof from slipping off.

batten

■ Assemble the box, nailing front, base, sides and back together, remembering to leave a gap at the bottom for the bats to enter (it should be large enough for your fingers, about 3cm/1¼in wide).

■ Finally, attach the roof, pressing it into the groove in the back plate.

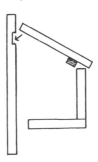

FIXING THE BOX

The box can be nailed onto a wooden post or tree, using the holes drilled earlier. If attaching to brickwork, use rawlplugs and screws.

AFTERCARE

At first, inspect the boxes regularly for droppings or other signs of habitation. Lift the roof very carefully, in case bats are inside. If there are bats, you must contact English Nature or the relevant Statutory Nature Conservation Organisation (SNCO) (addresses on page 141) to apply for a licence to continue checking.

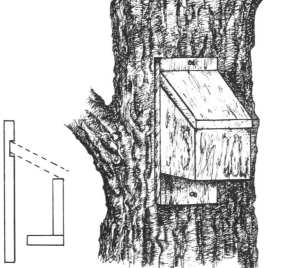

BAT SPECIES

COMMONLY SEEN IN GARDENS AND AROUND HOUSES:
Brown long-eared
Daubenton's (especially near ponds and canals)
Natterer's
Noctule
Pipistrelle
Serotine (especially in the south of England)

RARELY SEEN:
Barbastelle
Bechstein's
Brandt's
Greater and lesser horseshoe
Grey long-eared
Leisler's
Whiskered

EXTINCTION
In 1992 the mouse-eared bat, which had been struggling for survival for many years, finally became extinct in England – the first mammal to become extinct in the British Isles for 250 years.

THE LAW AND BATS
Bats and their roosts are protected by law and it is an offence to disturb roosting bats. If you have bats in the roof space, cellar or any other part of your property not used as a living area, you should contact the relevant SNCO as above.

FEBRUARY

Typically, this is a wet and bitterly cold month with more than its fair share of snow and ice. Fortunately, the weather does not make all wildlife inactive and in the early morning it is quite possible to see fox and badger tracks, made during the previous night, as they find mates and make preparations for the birth of their cubs.

Resident birds will also be gearing up for the breeding season. An early morning chorus of robins, blackbirds and thrushes signals the increasing interest males and females are taking in one another as they noisily advertise for mates. In a small garden it is unusual to have more than one pair of any particular species nesting, simply because the males will defend their territory against incomers of the same species. Even in mild weather birds are still reliant on supplementary food from the bird table, particularly the females who are building up their strength for breeding.

Frogs and toads are beginning to emerge from hibernation, although if the weather is extremely cold they will stay out of sight for another month. Butterflies, particularly brimstones and commas, may be stirred into life by a spell of weak sunshine. This is the month that catkins begin to appear on the branches of hazel and alder trees. Hazel catkins are known colloquially as 'lambs' tails', making a connection in our minds between the first sight of these flowers and the beginning of a new seasonal cycle. Beneath the trees, celandines, sweet violets, spring crocus and snowdrops are making a carpet of scent and colour, offering sustenance to waking insects and setting the scene for spring.

tasks

FOR THE

month

MOVING TREES AND SHRUBS
This is the last month for lifting and replanting shrubs or trees which may be in the wrong position. By spring, nest building will be underway, and moving established plants can be very disruptive. If the ground is too hard or the weather bad, leave until autumn.

CHECKLIST

- Continue feeding birds
- Prune *Buddleia davidii*
- Cut back overgrown berberis and cotoneaster
- Lift and divide perennial border plants
- Prune shrub roses
- Plant lily of the valley
- Trimming back perennials

FEEDING BIRDS

Continue putting out food and water on the bird table, particularly during cold spells. (See p12 for tips on feeding.) This is also a good month to put up nesting boxes that garden birds will use during the spring (see pp24-5).

PRUNING BUDDLEIA

Buddleia davidii bushes may be pruned this month. Strictly speaking, buddleia does not need to be pruned – witness the hundreds of thousands of garden escapees growing untended on urban wasteland. However, bushes which have outgrown their space or produced a poor show of flowers will benefit, producing strong new stems and, more importantly, large clusters of flowers for the butterflies.

- Cut back all last year's shoots to within 5 or 8cm (2 or 3in) of the old wood as shown.

- In mild winters, new rosettes of leaves may already have started to form at the junction of the old and new wood and

these should be left undamaged.

PRUNING BERBERIS AND COTONEASTER

Barberry (*Berberis*) and cotoneaster shrubs, both of value for their berries, can be cut back to prevent them becoming too overgrown and woody. The thicker, tougher three-year-old stems (or older) are cut out at ground level, opening up the plant to allow more light and air to the centre.

- Using sharp secateurs, prune the old wood back to within a few inches of the ground as shown.

LIFTING AND DIVIDING BORDER PERENNIALS

Hardy perennial plants which have been in place for three years or more can be lifted and divided now to make new plants. All the species listed are good for wildlife, and this is the simplest method of propagation. (Division can also be done in autumn.)

- Prepare the ground where the new plants are going to be put, by digging over and adding some garden compost.

- Using a fork, gently work the clump out of the ground, taking care not to break the roots.

- For large clumps, insert two forks, back to back, into the centre of the clump and prise the roots apart. Small clumps can be pulled apart by hand.

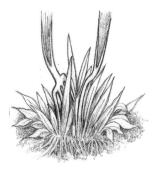

- Select small, healthy pieces from the outside of the plant with at least three or four young shoots, for replanting. The central woody portion can be discarded. The new sections can be planted immediately, allowing enough room between plants for development to their full size.

PRUNE SHRUB ROSES

The species shrub roses can be pruned now that the hips have been safely eaten during the winter months and while the plant is still dormant. Wild and species roses, whether grown as hedging or as shrubs, do not need annual hard pruning like the hybrid bush roses, but from time to time they will benefit from a light 'tidying up' – perhaps every three or four years. Dog rose *(Rosa canina)*, sweet briar *(Rosa rubiginosa)*, *Rosa rugosa*, *Rosa* x *alba*, and *Rosa*

glauca can all be treated in the same way.

- Using sharp secateurs, first cut out any old, dead or diseased stems at ground level.

- Cut back any long straggly stems to one third of their length to keep the plant tidy.

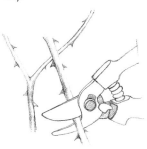

- Finally, snip off a few centimetres or inches from the tips of all the stems to encourage side shoots, which will bear flowers in later years.

PLANTING LILY OF THE VALLEY

Lily of the valley *(Convallaria majalis)*, best known for the delicious fragrance of its white, bell-shaped flowers, is so widely planted in gardens that it is sometimes forgotten that it is a native of our woodlands, although not so widespread in the wild as it used to be. It spreads rapidly if given the right conditions and makes an excellent woodland floor plant for a wild part of the garden. Existing clumps can be divided now or individual crowns can be bought from nurseries.

- Choose a shady spot with moist soil into which some leaf mould has been added.

- Plant the crowns point upwards, 8–10cm (3–4in) apart. They should lie just beneath the surface of the soil. Clumps of crowns can be placed 15cm (6in) apart.

- Water in well.

TRIMMING BACK PERENNIALS

Border perennial plants which were not cut back in autumn (leaving the stems for over-wintering insects) should be trimmed now to make room for new growth. Cut off any dead or straggly stems to just above ground level with secateurs.

In mild winters, young leaves and stems will already be appearing. Removing the old growth rejuvenates the plants and allows these new leaves and stems plenty of room to grow. Add the cuttings to the compost heap.

PERENNIALS TO DIVIDE

Globe thistle
(Echinops ritro) B, N
Golden rod
(Solidago canadensis) B, N
Greater knapweed
(Centaurea scabiosa) B, N, Nat
Michaelmas daisy
(Aster novi-belgii) N
Sedum
(S. spectabile and 'Autumn Joy')* N
Yarrow
(Achillea millefolium and
A. filipendulina) B, N, Nat

SHY-FLOWERING LILIES
One of the reasons lily of the valley often fails in gardens is that it is planted in dry, open, sunny beds, when it really needs a moist soil and the cover of deciduous trees.

plants
OF THE
month

and slower growing – more suitable for average-sized gardens

wildlife value There are around ninety insect species associated with alder, including the alder fly and alder moth. As the weather warms up the male catkins open and disperse a cloud of pollen to fertilise the female catkins. In autumn and winter the tree is a good source of seed for siskins, redpolls and other small birds

HAZEL
(*Corylus avellana*)

An ancient native shrub that forms thickets in the wild and bears the distinctive 'lambs'-tails' catkins and edible hazelnuts or cobnuts. Traditionally coppiced to produce flexible lengths for woven fencing and basket making.

type	Deciduous shrub
flowers	Catkins in late winter. Male catkins are yellow; female are tiny red tassels
height	4–6m (12–20ft)
spread	5m (15ft)
planting	Plant young trees between mid-autumn and early spring
site	Sunny or partly shaded. In a shrub border or amongst larger trees
soil	Any well-drained soil
care	No pruning required. If planted as part of a mini woodland, hazel can be coppiced (regularly cut back to ground level so that new straight shoots are sent out from the base), allowing more light to the woodland floor. In the autumn, nuts should be collected when the husks have turned brown and stored in a dry, airy place
propagation	By seed collected in the autumn
varieties	Corkscrew hazel (*C. avellana* 'Contorta') is a good alternative for a small garden. It has the same bright yellow catkins, but it is slow-growing and will only reach 2.5m (8ft) in height. The stems are twisted, hence the name
wildlife value	At this time of year, a gust of wind causes the catkins to release a cloud of pollen, for the benefit of early foraging bees and insects. In autumn the nuts are collected by squirrels and field mice, who add them to their winter store

ALDER
(*Alnus glutinosa*)

The tall-growing native alder is happiest beside a freshwater river or stream, but it is also very adaptable to garden sites. It is particularly useful in cities and towns because of its resistance to air pollution.

type	Deciduous tree
flowers	Catkins appear in late winter/early spring. Male catkins are long and yellow; females are round and purplish
height	10–15m (30–50ft)
spread	3m (10ft)
planting	Plant young trees from mid-autumn to early spring
site	In a marshy area or at the back of a woodland belt
soil	Prefers damp, waterlogged soil
care	No special care needed
propagation	From seed collected in autumn
varieties	*A. glutinosa* 'Imperialis' is smaller

STINKING HELLEBORE
(Helleborus foetidus)

The stinking hellebore earned its name from the seed pods which produce an acrid smell when crushed, although certainly not as unpleasant as the name suggests. It is quite a rare plant in the wild, although it can be found in old woodlands on chalky soils. The unusual pallid flowers and dramatic leaves make it an interesting garden plant and a useful supply of early nectar.

type	Perennial, evergreen
flowers	Yellow-green with purple rim, late winter to mid-spring
height	60cm (24in)
planting	Plant pot-grown plants in autumn
site	Shade
soil	Dry, chalky
care	Leave undisturbed
propagation	From seed in summer
related species	The green hellebore (*Helleborus viridis*) also flowers this month and can be distinguished by the wholly green flowers, without the purple edging. It is smaller, only 45cm (18in) high, and it prefers a moist soil. The leaves are deciduous, dying back in summer
wildlife value	Both hellebores are a ready source of nectar for early honey and bumble bees. *H. viridis* flowers a couple of weeks later than *H. foetidus*, so by planting both, a continuous supply of nectar is assured

SWEET VIOLET
(Viola odorata)

A widespread native flower, the sweet-smelling violet grows naturally on banks, in copses and in hedgerows. In the garden it will adapt to any shady location, in grass under trees, under hedges or in the border. Its relative, the common dog violet (*Viola riviniana*) is unscented and flowers later, but is also a useful wildlife plant, supplying nectar for spring broods of butterfly.

type	Perennial
flowers	Dark violet, sometimes white, late winter to mid-spring; occasionally in autumn
height	10–15cm (4–6in)
spread	30cm (12in)
planting	Plant out in early autumn or late spring, 30cm (12in) apart
site	Partial shade
soil	Any
care	No special care needed
propagation	Plants spread naturally by runners. These can be rooted in summer or the whole plant can be divided in autumn
varieties	A range of colours are available in the garden varieties; 'Coeur d'Alsace' is a rich pink and 'Sulphurea' is a yellow form
wildlife value	This is the earliest flowering of the native violets and provides nectar for flying insects and food for butterfly caterpillars, particularly the fritillary family

SHRINKING VIOLETS
*The population of some species of violet is dwindling, so it is vital to buy seeds and young plants from nurseries and not to collect from the wild. The Teesdale violet (*V. nepestris*) is found only in Upper Teesdale and at a single site in Cumbria. Likewise, the fen violet (*V. persicifolia*) is confined to a few scattered locations in East Anglia*

practical project

MAKING AND SITING NEST BOXES

A RANGE OF BOXES FOR A RANGE OF BIRDS

Simple wall ledge for blackbirds, sparrows, spotted flycatchers, thrushes
Dimensions: 15x15cm (6x6in)
Open-fronted box for pied wagtails, robins, spotted flycatchers, wrens
Dimensions: 15cm (6in) wide x 15cm (6in) deep
Log box for sparrows, tits, wrens
Standard box for sparrows, tits, wrens
Dimensions: 15cm (6in) wide x 15cm (6in) deep; hole 30mm (1½in) maximum diameter
Open-fronted owl/kestrel box for kestrels site as high as possible; for owls site inside a disused building
Dimensions: 45cm (18in) wide x 45cm (18in) deep x 40cm (16in) high

Birds need safe places to raise their young in the spring and summer, and gardens provide some of the best habitats. If possible there should be a choice of potential sites that different species can use – thick hedgerows for sparrows, walls covered by climbers for blackbirds and thrushes, hollow tree trunks for blue tits, sheds and outbuildings for robins and swallows. Nest boxes should be thought of as an adjunct to these natural sites, not a replacement for them. In towns, where trees are scarce, or in brand new gardens, nest boxes are vital and it is worth trying to include several types in different positions.

CHOOSING A BOX

The type of bird you want to attract will determine the type of nesting box – anything from a simple wooden ledge to a large owl box. The ones made from wood, in natural colours, are preferable as they will not advertise the birds' location to potential predators. Some shops and garden centres sell combined nest box and feeding tables. This is a nice idea but it is also very unlikely that a bird would nest in such a prominent position.

SITING THE BOX

Try to put it in view of a window, so you can watch the occupants without disturbing them. It should be put at least 3m (10ft) from the ground, out of reach of cats and other predators. Walls are safer than trees to some degree as cats find them difficult to climb. Try the boxes at different heights to see which species use them. Some birds, like

TYPES OF NESTING BOXES

SIMPLE WALL LEDGE — OPEN-FRONTED BOX — LOG BOX

STANDARD BOX — OPEN-FRONTED OWL/KESTREL BOX

45cm (18in)	11.2cm (4½in)	21.2cm (8½in)	20cm (8in)	25cm (10in)	20cm (8in)	15cm (6in)
back	base	roof	front	side	side	

← 1.5ft (5ft) →

kestrels, naturally nest at roof-top level or even higher. Make sure all boxes face north, east or south-east, to avoid strong sun and driving rain.

CONSTRUCTING THE NEST BOX

■ Use a plank of untreated wood (old floor-boards or skirting boards for example) 2cm (¾in) thick, 15cm (6in) wide by 1.5m (5ft) long and mark up as shown above.

■ Saw the plank into the required pieces and make the entrance hole using a drill. The hole should be around 2.5–3cm (1–1¼in) wide.

■ Drill two holes into the back plate, top and bottom, to enable it to be attached to the tree.

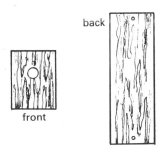

back

front

■ Nail or screw the box together as shown, all except the lid.

■ Attach the lid to the box with a strip of leather or rubber to form a hinge and to keep out the rain. The lid can be secured at each side with small metal hooks.

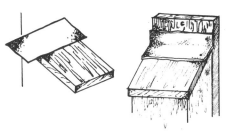

FIXING THE BOX

■ Nail the box to a wooden post or tree or attach to brickwork using rawlplugs and screws. Boxes can also be hung from strong branches, using wires as shown.

AFTERCARE

Once a pair of birds has adopted the box, it should not be inspected or disturbed. Although it is tempting to keep checking on the progress of eggs and chicks, you risk frightening off the parents altogether. Instead keep a watch on the box and note down which species used it and when. Note also when the young birds leave the box, as they may return to roost there for a few weeks after leaving. In some years, a pair of birds will rear more than one brood.

In the autumn, when you are certain the box has been vacated, clear out the old nesting material which can harbour parasites.

Pied wagtail

READY-MADE NEST BOXES
Ready-made boxes and detailed plans for making a range of specialised nest boxes can be obtained from the Royal Society for the Protection of Birds (RSPB) and the British Trust for Ornithology (BTO) (addresses on page 141)

MARCH

This is a time of great activity in the garden, as the weather softens and many species of wildlife begin their breeding cycles. In warmer areas frogs will have already laid their spawn, but in others the noisy calls of the males indicate that mating is still under way.

Toads usually spawn later than frogs and newts last of all. Toad spawn is easily identifiable as the long double strands of eggs, as opposed to the frogs' clumps of jelly and the newts' eggs laid singly on pondweed. There are many threats to the developing young which may prevent them reaching maturity, but perhaps the greatest loss is the large number of adult toads killed each year by cars, as they migrate across roads to their traditional breeding ponds.

Mammals tend to be out of sight this month with fox and badger cubs being born underground. Birds are also busy building nests and defending their territories against intruders. Nesting material is drawn from a wide variety of garden sources, including grass stems, strips of bark, dead leaves and moss taken from the lawn. A slightly unkempt garden or one with a good compost heap is a richer source of nesting material than one which is clinically neat and tidy.

*The onset of spring is signalled by a flush of yellow flowers. The vivid yellows of celandines, narcissus and primula seem to act as a beacon to insects emerging from hibernation to seek pollen. The true wild daffodil (*Narcissus pseudonarcissus*) is generally later to emerge than the garden species and may not appear until next month. It is smaller and less ostentatious than its hybridised cousins and perfectly suited to the wildlife garden.*

tasks

FOR THE

month

INTRODUCING FROGS AND
TOADS
If the garden pond has no
amphibians, it is possible to
'import' frog, toad or newt spawn
from other ponds. This is the only
way to increase the population
as it is inadvisable to move
tadpoles and quite cruel to move
adults from their home pond.
Take a bucketful of water, pond
weed and spawn from a
neighbouring pond. It is best to
take more than you need as
some batches of spawn will not
survive the change of water
temperature.

BIRD FEEDING

Unless the weather is particularly harsh, reduce feeding as nesting begins. Hard bread and peanuts are harmful to newly hatched birds, so restrict food supplies to soft fat or grated cheese. Reducing the amount of food supplied will encourage the adults to start feeding on the emerging insects. However, if the ground is frozen, keep up the feeding until the bad weather passes.

DEALING WITH WEEDS

Perennial flower and shrub borders should be checked now for weeds and unwanted seedlings. Perennial weeds like ground elder will need to be dug out thoroughly as even the tiniest section of root left in the soil can sprout again. Annual weeds can be dealt with more easily, by disturbing only the top layer of soil. Use a garden fork (or hand fork) to lift them out of the soil, pulling the plant and stem cleanly away.

MULCHING

To suppress further weeds

from growing, cover the soil with a layer of mulch. This can be any material that excludes light from the soil, thus preventing weeds from growing. Black polythene or old carpet will suppress weeds and conserve the moisture already in the ground, although neither looks particularly attractive. A 5–8cm (2–3in) layer of chopped bark gives a natural woodland floor finish and birds do not seem to mind scattering the pieces to find insects. Another alternative is garden compost, which has the added bonus of releasing its nutrients into the soil throughout the spring and summer. These mulches will prevent the need to use chemical weedkillers and cut down on watering later in the summer.

DIVIDING MARGINAL POND AND WETLAND PLANTS

In established ponds, marginal species can outgrow their space in the shallow water around the edge and need to be renewed by division. Spring is the best time to do this, just as the plants are starting their growth.

Dividing clump-forming plants
This method applies to

marsh marigold *(Caltha palustris)* and most other moisture-loving perennials.

- Marginal plants that grow in clumps or mounds can be broken up simply with a hand fork. Lift the plant out of the soil or water and, using the fork, prise away small clumps from the outside of the main clump. Choose young, healthy-looking parts of the plant and discard the interior which may have become exhausted.

- Replant the new pieces immediately, into other parts of the pond. If not needed immediately, they can be grown on in pots of wet compost.

Dividing creeping plants
This method applies to flowering rush *(Butomus umbellatus)*, bog bean *(Menyanthes trifoliata)*, bog arum *(Calla palustris)*, water mint *(Mentha aquatica)* and lesser celandine *(Ranunculus ficaria)*. The roots of these plants have a scrambling habit and can be increased by dividing the horizontal rootstock into sections.

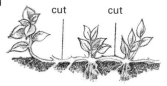

cut   cut

■ Remove the plant from the water and cut the rootstock into short sections. Each should have a healthy bud or young shoot and preferably a trace of roots attached.

■ On flowering rush, look for a small bulb-like formation (bulbil) at the point where the leaves meet the hard woody rootstock. Make sure each section includes a bulbil.

■ Plant these sections in trays of wet compost until they root and form healthy young plants.

CLIPPING FLOWERING HEATHER AND LAVENDER

The dead flowerheads of the summer-flowering heather *(Calluna vulgaris)* and scented lavender *(Lavandula)* can be clipped now to make way for new growth. Use a pair of garden shears and trim off the straggly dry stems, taking care not to cut into the woody parts. Both plants are valuable for bees, while heather also attracts a range of other insects and provides good cover for birds, insects and reptiles.

SOWING HALF-HARDY ANNUALS

Some of the summer garden nectar flowers, such as petunias and African

marigolds, are not fully hardy and need to be sown indoors this month. (Alternatively they may be bought as bedding plants in late spring, see page 52). It is not necessary to have a greenhouse to sow half-hardy annuals from seed and they can be successfully raised in the house.

■ Fill 8cm (3in) pots (or seed trays) with proprietary seed compost. Water the compost using a watering-can with a fine-spray rose and allow pots to drain before sowing. Firm down the compost to a flat surface, using the base of another pot.

■ Sow the seed thinly on the surface of the compost, spacing it out as evenly as possible. Cover larger seeds with a 1cm (1¼in) layer of sieved compost. Fine seeds do not need to be covered.

■ Label the pots and cover each one with a small polythene bag, securing it with a rubber band or just folding it underneath the pot.

■ Place the pots in a warm place, out of direct sunlight: an airing cupboard, shaded windowsill or greenhouse propagator. Open the plastic bags daily to release any built-up moisture, and check for signs of germination. When the first signs of growth appear (usually in one to three weeks), remove the plastic bags and move the pots to a lighter position – a windowsill or greenhouse bench. Water occasionally if the compost dries out.

■ When three or more leaves have appeared, carefully separate the seedlings and transfer them to individual pots. They can now be left to grow on until planting out in the garden in late spring or early summer, when the danger of frost is passed.

NECTAR FLOWERS TO SOW INDOORS

African marigold *(Tagetes erecta)*
French marigold *(Tagetes patula)*
Heliotrope *(Heliotropium)*
Petunia
Tobacco plant *(Nicotiana)*

Clipping lavender

plants
OF THE
month

POLLEN COUNT
It is not only flying insects and butterflies that are attracted to the pollen in spring flowers. Small mammals like voles and woodmice will seek out pollen as a source of protein.

WOOD ANEMONE
(Anemone nemorosa)

The wood anemone or 'wind flower' is a native of woodland, hedgerows and copses and makes a good, if somewhat rampant, garden plant.

type	Perennial, rhizomes
flowers	White, flushed with pink, spring
height	15–20cm (6–8in)
planting	Plant rhizomes in autumn, 5cm (2in) deep and 15cm (6in) apart
site	Sun or partial shade, under deciduous trees, hedges or in woodland clearings
soil	Any well-drained fertile soil
care	No special care needed
propagation	Spreads rapidly by underground rhizomes. Divide rhizomes in late summer after foliage has died back
related species	*Anemone blanda*, derived from a Greek wildflower, is widely grown in gardens for its blue or mauve flowers which are particularly attractive to bee flies. The yellow wood anemone *(A. ranunculoides)* may also be naturalised in shady areas
wildlife value	The wood anemone relies on bees and flies for its pollination and many flying insects actively seek out the flowers when they appear in spring

CROCUS

The vast array of garden hybrid crocuses start flowering in late winter and bring some welcome colour. Easily naturalised in grass or in flower beds they will take care of themselves and give a reliable show year after year.

type	Bulb
flowers	Purple, mauve, white, yellow, late winter to mid-spring
height	8cm (3in)
planting	Plant bulbs in early autumn, 8cm (3in) deep and 10cm (4in) apart
site	Sun or shade. In grass, under trees, in beds or rockeries
soil	Any, but prefers well drained
care	When grown in a lawn, leave the grass uncut until the leaves have died down
propagation	Lift established plants as soon as the leaves turn brown. Leave to dry, then remove the largest offsets and replant
related species	*C. tomasinianus* is a purple crocus, good for growing in grass. *C. chrysanthus* hybrids come in every shade of yellow, making eye-catching clumps in pots or beds. The true spring crocus (*C. vernus*) can be found naturalised in scattered parts of Britain although it does not come into flower until mid spring
wildlife value	A flock of sparrows can demolish a bed of crocuses in no time at all. Bees will also seek out the pollen on warm days

LESSER CELANDINE

 ## LESSER CELANDINE
(Ranunculus ficaria)

An abundant member of the buttercup family, the lesser celandine is found growing wild in woodlands and hedgerows, by streams and in damp hollows. It tends to spread rapidly in the right conditions, so should only be planted where there is enough room for it not to become troublesome.

type	Perennial, tuber
flowers	Bright yellow, early to late spring
height	10cm (4in)

planting	Plant between early autumn and late winter, burying the tuberous roots 5cm (2in) deep
site	Full or partial shade, in woodlands, ditches, hedgerows, wetlands
soil	Any, moist
care	No special care needed
propagation	Divide and replant in mid-autumn or early spring. Spreads very easily
wildlife value	Relies on insects, particularly flies and bees, for its pollination. Early source of nectar and pollen

practical project

MAKING A WILDLIFE POND

Probably the single most useful thing gardeners can do for wildlife is to make a pond. The traditional brick or concrete steep-sided structure is not really suitable, although any water in the garden is better than none. The best design is a shallow contoured pool which will allow access to a range of creatures. Water is essential for frogs, toads and newts who will use it to breed. It is also useful as a drinking station for hedgehogs and foxes and as a bathing area for birds. A good range of insects specific to water and marsh habitats will use the pond, including dragonflies, damselflies, water spiders and water boatmen. It will also become a breeding ground for midges which are an important food source for bats, swifts and swallows through the summer months.

WHERE TO SITE THE POND

Choose a sunny position, on level ground and away from overhanging trees. If the water might be a danger to young children, it should be positioned well away from the house and, if necessary, fenced off. Make use of any natural hollows in the land to reduce the amount of digging needed, although it is best to avoid those which already have water in them as further excavation would be difficult. It is a good idea to place one side of the pond adjacent to a border of low-growing shrubs or dense planting. As new frogs hatch in spring, they need cover to escape being eaten by birds. In any case, one side of the pond should be made inaccessible to human feet, to give pond wildlife an undisturbed area.

Water spider

SIZE

Make the pond as large as space will allow, but at least 3m (10ft) square. With smaller ponds it is difficult to make the sides slope gently enough and it is harder to maintain a healthy balance of plants and water creatures. At some point the pond should be 75cm (2ft 6in) deep to prevent complete freezing in winter.

CONSTRUCTING THE POND

Use a flexible butyl rubber liner. There are cheaper alternatives available, and if choosing one of these, make sure it has a guarantee of at least ten years' life. The size of the liner needed can be calculated using the following formula:

Liner width = Pond width +
(2 × max pond depth) + 30cm (12in)
Liner length = Pond length +
(2 × max pond depth) + 30cm (12in)

The extra 30cm (12in) is necessary to allow for an overlap all around the edge.

■ Mark out the shape of the pond using a flexible hosepipe, rope or short canes. Rounded curves look more natural than angular shapes. For a small pond, tight curves will be difficult to dig, so choose a simple oval shape. Large ponds can be lagoon, figure-of-eight or pear-shaped.

■ Remove a strip of turf (or soil), 30cm (12in) wide and 5–8cm (2–3in) deep all the way around the edge of the pond, outside the shape marked. Lay the turves aside for later use.

■ Start to dig the pond within the marked area, starting from the outside and working in. Remove turf, soil and stones, making a series of shelves and gentle slopes. For marginal plants, a shelf at about 23cm (9in) deep is useful.

■ When the contouring of the soil inside the pond is complete, pat down the soil and re-

Use a hosepipe to mark out the pond area

Remove a strip of turf all round the outside of the pond

23cm (9in)

sand

When digging the pond, create a shelf for marginal plants

Water boatman

Ease the liner into position and anchor with stones

move any sharp stones. Lay a plank of wood across the pond (widthways and lengthways) and, using a spirit level, make a final check that the sides are level.

■ Put a 5–8cm (2–3in) layer of damp builders' sand over the soil to give extra protection to the liner. Pat the sand down firmly to the contours of the pond. Old carpet, carpet underlay or sheets of wet cardboard can be used instead.

■ Unfold the liner over the hole and ease it into position. Anchor the outside edge using stones. A pile of smooth stones can also be put at the deepest part ot hold the liner in position and may be left in place after the pool is filled. *(Continued on p36)*

LINKING A MARSH OR WETLAND AREA TO THE POND

It is possible to incorporate a marshy area linked to the main pond. When excavating the pond, an additional shallow area is dug, divided from the rest of the pond by a line of heavy stones. The area is backfilled with soil and as the water level in the pond rises, water percolates into the marsh area and drains back into the pond.

In practice, this can be a rather tricky feature to get right, and in many ponds the earth tends to be drawn back into the pond or, conversely, the water is sucked out of the pond and into the marsh. In this case it might be a better idea to make an independent wetland garden (see page 44).

M A R C H

plants
OF THE
month

 ### FLOWERING CURRANT
(Ribes sanguineum)

Not a native plant, but the bees flock to the deep pink flowers of *R. sanguineum* as soon as they open. It goes on flowering for several months – longer than most other exotic garden shrubs.

type	Deciduous shrub
flowers	Deep rose-red, spring
height	1.8–2.5m (6–8ft)
spread	1.5–2.2m (5–7ft)
planting	Container-grown shrubs can be planted at any time, although late autumn or early spring gives young plants the best chance of success
site	Sun or light shade, shrub border
soil	Any well-drained soil
care	Apply a mulch of garden compost or manure in spring. Cut out any old wood at ground level as soon as possible after flowering
propagation	By hardwood cuttings in autumn
wildlife value	*R. sanguineum* is attractive to early bees and one of the best sources of spring nectar. Sparrows and tits also use the bush for picking off aphids

PRIMROSE
(Primula vulgaris)

The wild primrose is the first of the native primulas to emerge and arguably the prettiest. Naturally found on damp, heavy soils in woods, coppices and hedgebanks, it has greatly declined in recent years due to the loss of suitable habitats and overpicking. In gardens it has been replaced by hybrids (particularly with polyanthus) which produce showy, double pink and coloured forms – a far cry from the simple, pale yellow *P. vulgaris*.

type	Perennial
flowers	Pale yellow, early to mid-spring
height	15cm (6in)
planting	Plant seedlings 23cm (9in) apart in autumn or early spring
site	Sun or partial shade, in woodland, under hedges or shrubs, by ponds or streams or in a damp, spring-flowering meadow
soil	Moist, fertile soil
care	Mulch ground around plants in spring, if necessary, to retain moisture
propagation	By division after flowering (late spring) or by seed sown in early summer
related species	The primrose's closest relatives are the cowslip *(P. veris)* and the oxlip *(P. elatior)* (see p47). There is also a rare, dark purple primrose *(P. scotica)*, found only on the northern coasts of Scotland
wildlife value	As a threatened species, the primrose may be grown simply for conservation reasons, but it is also a useful source of nectar for spring butterflies, particularly the 'whites'

PRIMROSE

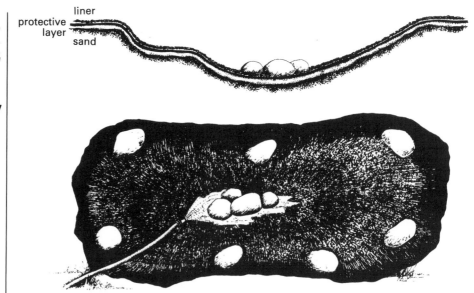

liner
protective layer
sand

Fill the pond via a hosepipe

practical project

MAKING A WILDLIFE POND

PLANTS FOR THE POND

NATIVE OXYGENATORS
Curled pondweed
(Potamogeton crispus)
Hornwort
(Ceratophyllum demersum)
Spiked water milfoil
(Myriophyllum spicatum)
Water starwort
(Callitriche stagnalis)

HABIT
Fully submerged, although flowers often appear just above the surface.

PLANTING
Plant bunches in soil in deepest part of the pond. Anchor with bricks or rock until established. Oxygenators increase rapidly so introduce only a few bunches at first – as a guide, allow four to five bunches for a .3m (10ft) square pond.

AVOID OVERPLANTING
Don't be tempted to cram too many plants into a small water area. A balanced pool needs areas of open water, as well as margins of dense planting.

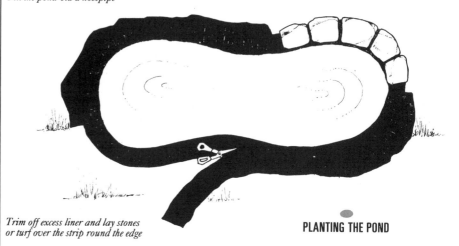

Trim off excess liner and lay stones or turf over the strip round the edge

■ Over the butyl liner, put another protective layer, such as polyester matting (sold in garden centres as an under layer), plus a layer of poor garden soil (riddled to get rid of stones) or a sand-and-gravel mixture. This serves two functions, as a protection for the liner and as a rooting medium for the plants. Don't use compost or rich soil which contains too many nutrients.

■ Fill the pond, using tapwater via a hose. As the pond fills up, ease off the edges of the liner as necessary by removing the stones.

■ Trim off any excess liner, and finish the pond by laying turf or paving stones over the 30cm (12in) strip around the edge.

PLANTING THE POND

Leave the water to settle for a week or two before beginning planting. Early spring is a good time to start planting, but in fact plants can be put in right through the summer and into early autumn.

The aim is to include as many native species as possible and to select a range of plants with different habits of growth. Oxygenating plants grow underwater and help to keep the water clean. They also support an incredible variety of microscopic creatures and provide food for water snails. Aquatic plants with floating leaves, like water lilies, shade parts of the water from the sun, which in turn controls algae growth. The leaves are also used as convenient stepping stones for amphibians and small birds. Marginal plants thrive in shallow water at the edges of the pond and form the link between the pond and the rest of the garden. These plants, with most of their stems, leaves and flowers out of the water, provide cover for young frogs and toads. The taller species are particularly important for dragonflies, who lay their eggs on the stems.

NOTE

■ *For small ponds, the fringed water lily is a better choice than the gigantic white lily which can cover the entire water surface* ■

ATTRACTING WILDLIFE TO THE POND

Many water creatures will be introduced to the pond when the plants are put in, including water snails who lay their eggs on the underside of large-leaved plants like lilies. Many flying insects will colonise the water without being introduced, particularly pond skaters and dragonflies. It also helps to add a bucketful of sludge or mud from a well-established pond to help the process along.

Frogs, toads and newts should be introduced in spring as spawn and not as adults. Try to get recently laid spawn from an overstocked pond. If there are no suitable ponds nearby, contact the local wildlife trust for advice (via the RSNC – address page 141).

WARNING

■ *Avoid Canadian Pondweed* (Elodea canadensis) – *although commonly sold in garden centres it tends to swamp all other vegetation and is difficult to control* ■

POND MANAGEMENT

The best pond management system is to leave it alone as much as possible. Ponds take time to reach an equilibrium and attempts to speed this up by using chemicals to clear the water will result in a serious imbalance.

The most frequent pond problem is the build-up of algae and pondweed. Both are usually kept under control by a healthy population of native water snails and, if necessary, extra supplies can be bought from pet stores. (Beware of buying imported varieties which might wipe out the indigenous species.) Too much algae is also an indicator that the water is too rich in nutrients. To counteract this, top up the pond with rainwater instead of tapwater and never add compost or garden soil which contains fertilisers. Another way of reducing the build-up of nutrients is to remove some of the vegetation in late summer or early autumn.

ADAPTING A FORMAL POND FOR WILDLIFE

Formal ponds can be adapted to the needs of wildlife without the need to build a whole new structure.
■ Phase out ornamental fish, which will eat tadpoles.
■ Add 'steps' to counteract the steep sides and make it easier for birds, amphibians and small mammals to get access to shallow water. A series of bricks or large rocks can form a link between the deepest part of the pool and the edge.
■ Soften the edges of the pond with marginal planting to provide cover for frogs and toads. Prop planting baskets on bricks if the water is too deep.
■ Introduce more native species, gradually replacing exotic plants with their native equivalents, to increase the range of insects using the plants for breeding and feeding.

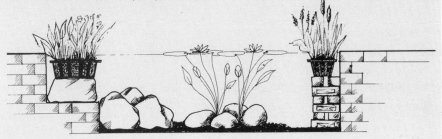

NATIVE FLOATING-LEAVED PLANTS
Amphibious bistort
(Polygonum amphibium)
Common water crowfoot
(Ranunculus aquatilis)
Fringed water lily (Nymphoides peltata)
Frogbit
(Hydrocharis morsus-ranae)
White water lily
(Nymphaea alba)

HABIT
Root on the bottom, but leaves and flowers float on the surface of the water.

PLANTING
Anchor individual plants in soil with heavy stones until well established.

NATIVE MARGINALS
Bog bean (Menyanthes trifoliata)
PD = 15–45cm (6–18in)
Flowering rush
(Butomus umbellatus)
PD = 8–15cm (3–6in)
Lesser reedmace
(Typha angustifolia), W
PD = 8–15cm (3–6in) or wet soil
Lesser spearwort
(Ranunculus flammula), W
PD = 8–15cm (3–6in) or wet soil
Marsh marigold
(Caltha palustris), W
PD = 0–8cm (0–3in) or wet soil
Water mint (Mentha aquatica), W
PD = 0–8cm (0–3in) or wet soil
Yellow flag iris
(Iris pseudacorus)
PD = 0–15cm (0–6in)

HABIT
Grow in shallow water towards the edges of the pond, with most of the stem, leaves and flowers above water. Those marked W will grow in shallow water or wet soil and are suitable for the wetland garden (see p44-5.)

PLANTING
Plant directly into the soil on shelves or gentle slopes within the optimum depth range.

KEY
PD = Planting depth, the depth of water above the soil level

APRIL

This is the month of showers and sun, of unpredictable weather and bursts of new growth. Deciduous climbers, which it seemed would never be green, are covered in new shoots once again. Bulbs, planted in hope last autumn, emerge right on cue, triggered by their infallible timeclock mechanism locked underground. Frosts and unexpected snow flurries may interrupt the march of spring, but any setbacks are only temporary. The surge of new life can only be slowed down, never stopped altogether.

The breeding season for garden birds is in full swing and every available nest box, hedge and dense climber will be occupied. In ideal conditions, most birds would prefer to site their nest a respectful distance from their neighbours, but in urban areas, where suitable sites are precious, it is quite possible to see birds of different species nesting in close proximity. This is also the time that summer migrants return from the African continent to breed, some in huge numbers like the willow warblers, housemartins, swifts and swallows. Other visitors are less common, such as the pied flycatcher which settles in old, deciduous woods only in western Britain. Here it will build a nest almost exclusively from strips of bark taken from the wild honeysuckle, which makes up the shrubby underlayer of these woods.

Some of the mammals born underground last month will now have their eyes open and be ready to leave the nest. In an undisturbed part of the garden it is quite possible to find tiny wood mice, shrews or field voles under a pile of logs or a sheet of corrugated iron. When they do venture out, they will be easy prey for larger birds like kestrels. Fox and badger cubs may emerge on warm evenings later in the month, although the parents will try to keep them underground for as long as they can contain the cubs' natural curiosity and instinct for exploration.

tasks

FOR THE

month

RECOMMENDED HARDY ANNUALS

Candytuft *(Iberis umbellata)* N
Clarkia *(Clarkia elegans)* B, C
California poppy
(Eschscholzia californica) N, B, H
Corncockle
(Agrostemma githago) Nat, N, Po
Corn chamomile
(Anthemis arvensis) Nat, N
Cornflower
(Centaurea cyanus) Nat, N, B
Larkspur
(Delphinium consolida) Nat, B, Po
Love-in-a-mist
(Nigella damascena) N, B
Mignonette *(Reseda odorata)* N
Nasturtium
(Tropaeolum majus) C, H
Night-scented stock
(Matthiola bicornis) N, M
Poached egg flower
(Limnanthes douglasii) B, H, N
Pot marigold
(Calendula officinalis) B,H, N
Sunflower
(Helianthus annuus) N, B, S
Virginia stock
(Malcolmia maritima) N

CHECKLIST

☐ Put away the bird table
☐ Sow hardy annual seeds outdoors
☐ First cut of new flowering meadow
☐ Plant pond and wetland plants
☐ Plant climbers and put up trellis

BIRD TABLE

The bird table can be put away now and stored for next winter. Wash down the surfaces with a mild disinfectant and water to remove all traces of food and droppings.

SOW HARDY ANNUAL SEEDS

As the weather improves, many annual garden and wildflowers can be sown outdoors. This is one of the cheapest and easiest ways to provide flowering nectar plants for the garden's insects and is ideal for anyone starting a garden from scratch. By choosing hardy species that won't be harmed by any unexpectedly cold weather, the seeds can be sown directly into the ground where they are intended to grow and do not need to be nursed in greenhouses or coldframes.

■ Prepare the soil by lightly forking over, removing any large stones or clods of earth. Water thoroughly.

■ Sprinkle the seeds by hand over the whole area.

■ Rake in the seeds to make sure they are just buried.

■ If there is no rain for a day or two after sowing, water the ground with a fine-rose watering can, making sure the water soaks deeply into the soil.

Aftercare
Remove any competing weed seedlings as they come up between the flowers. When they only

have two or three pairs of leaves it is difficult to tell the difference, so wait until the plants are easily recognisable. Thin out any groups of plants that are overcrowded, by removing some of the seedlings. Continue to water annual beds throughout the summer, particularly in hot, dry spells.

CUTTING THE NEW FLOWERING MEADOW

New wildflower lawns or meadows, sown the previous autumn, should have their first cut when the grass reaches a height of 10cm (4in) (see p104-5). This is only applicable to lawns sown with a standard grass and perennial flower mixture and not those containing annual flowers which are cut in late summer.

Before mowing, roll the lawn lightly to make sure the seedlings are securely bedded in the soil. Use a heavy duty rotary mower or motor-scythe, and cut at a height of 5–8cm (2–3in). (These machines can be hired by the day from local tool-hire shops.) A sharp hand scythe also cuts the grass efficiently, but should only be handled by people trained in its use. Leave the cuttings in place for a day or two to allow any creatures to crawl back into the meadow, then rake off and add to the compost heap.

PLANTING WATER AND WETLAND PLANTS

Spring is a good time to put in container-grown pond plants, although they can be planted at any time between now and late autumn. Select a place in the pond with the right depth of water, according to the growing preferences of the plant (see page 37 for plant lists). Gently insert the roots into the soil or growing medium in the pond. Place a small stone on top of the root ball to secure the plant until the roots start to anchor themselves. At this time of year growth is rapid and new plants should establish easily.

PLANTING CLIMBERS

Spring is a good time to put in new climbers, giving them a chance of making enough growth to cover a wall or fence by the end of the season. For wildlife, the main consideration is to ensure that there is a gap between the flat surface and the climber itself, making a secluded enclave for nesting or roosting.

The usual framework for non-clinging plants (ie

everything except ivy and creepers) is a wooden trellis or horizontal wires. Instead of nailing the trellis flat against the wall, small wooden battens are screwed to the wall first, to hold the trellis several centimetres or a few inches away. Similarly, the 'eyes' which hold the wires can be attached to the battens rather than being put straight into the wall.

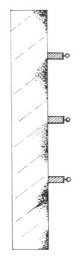

Planting container-grown climbers
■ Water the plant well in its pot. Carefully detach the top growth from its support, removing wires, ties or canes.

NOTE

■ *Container-grown climbers can be planted at any time of the year, although it is best to avoid mid-summer and mid-winter* ■

■ Dig a hole 30cm (12in) away from the wall. It should be as deep as and slightly wider than the container. (The plant should sit in the hole so that the surface of the compost is level with the surrounding soil.)

■ Mix a little garden compost or well-rotted manure with the soil taken from the hole and add a spadeful to the bottom of the hole. Remove the plant from its container and place in the hole.

■ Fill around the roots with the soil mixture, treading down firmly. Water thoroughly, making sure the water soaks right down around the roots.

RECOMMENDED CLIMBING PLANTS

Ceanothus
(C. x burkwoodii), N, E
aspect – south, west

Cotoneaster
(C. horizontalis), B, F
aspect – north, east

Firethorn
(Pyracantha), N, F, E
aspect – north, east

Honeysuckle
(Lonicera periclymenum), Nat, N, B
bark for nests
aspect – east, west

Ivy (Hedera helix), Nat, N, B, CF
aspect – north, east, west

Old man's beard
(Clematis vitalba), Nat, N
any aspect

Russian vine (Fallopia aubertii)
any aspect

All these climbers may be used as nesting sites for birds and possibly for bat roosts as well.

plants
OF THE
month

NATIVE SPRING BULBS

Common grape hyacinth
(Muscari neglectum)
English bluebell *(Scilla non-scripta)*
Ramsons garlic *(Allium ursinum)*
Snakeshead fritillary
(Fritillaria meleagris)
Wild daffodil
(Narcissus pseudonarcissus)
Spring crocus *(Crocus vernus)*

 ENGLISH BLUEBELL
(Scilla non-scripta)

The native bluebell is found growing in open woodlands, on grass banks and heaths. The old coppiced woodlands which suited it so well are declining and so natural colonies are becoming rare, but as a garden flower it is not at all difficult to establish.

type	Perennial bulb
flowers	Violet-blue (occasionally white or pink), mid-spring to early summer
height	30cm (12in)
planting	Plant bulbs in groups in early autumn, 10–15cm (4–6in) deep and 15cm (6in) apart. Bulbs do not store well, so plant as soon as possible after purchase
site	Sun or partial shade. Bluebells prefer some shade from the summer sun, under deciduous trees, or hedges
soil	Moist, with plenty of organic matter, such as leaf mould. Will tolerate drier conditions
care	Leave undisturbed if possible
propagation	Bluebells self-seed easily, but can also be increased by division. Lift clumps after leaves have died down, divide the bulbs and replant the offsets immediately
related species	The Spanish bluebell *(S. hispanica)* is widely grown and has escaped and become naturalised in some parts of Britain. The flowers are more erect than those of the native species and it is available in a wider range of colours
wildlife value	Many early insects will visit the bluebell for nectar, but its real value in the wildlife garden is for conservation of an irreplaceable wild plant

WILD DAFFODIL
(Narcissus pseudonarcissus)

Also known as the Lent lily, the wild daffodil is smaller and less conspicuous than its garden counterparts. Its natural habitat is meadows and deciduous woodlands, where it carpets the ground in drifts of colour. In the garden it may be naturalised in grass and under trees.

type	Bulb, perennial
flowers	Cream to pale yellow, mid-spring

height	15–30cm (6–12in)
planting	Plant bulbs in autumn, 8cm (3in) deep
site	In sun or partial shade, under deciduous trees or hedges, or in grass
soil	Any ordinary garden soil
care	Prefers to remain undisturbed. Clumps which become over-crowded or flower poorly may need to be lifted and divided
propagation	Divide bulbs only after they have been growing *in situ* for several years. Lift clumps in early summer, remove healthy offsets and replant immediately
wildlife value	*N. pseudonarcissus* is becoming less widespread in the wild, as more cultivated varieties escape (or are planted) on road verges and open spaces. Naturalised colonies in gardens may ensure its future survival

WILD DAFFODIL

practical project

MAKING AND PLANTING A WETLAND/MARSH

WETLAND WILDLIFE

Orange tip butterflies

Frogs and toads

Bats

Swifts, swallows and housemartins

Slow worms

Bees

Hoverflies

Undoubtedly one of the most fragile natural environments, wetlands are under threat from development in many areas of the country, indeed the world. This applies as much to the flood plains and water meadows bordering inconspicuous streams and rivers as it does to the major coastal estuaries. Even within our largest cities, small areas of wetland or marsh still exist and need to be identified and protected. They may be home to some spectacular wildlife – short-eared owls, for example – and also some very ordinary plants like reedmace, sedge and meadowsweet, which are no less interesting for being commonplace.

An area of wetland or marsh is a good way of extending the range of habitats available to wildlife in the garden. Many plants prefer a waterlogged soil rather than shallow water and they include some of our prettiest native flowers. Species like ragged robin are becoming increasingly rare in the wild and rely on garden cultivation for their future survival. Wetlands have their own balance of plants and creatures which is related though different to the pool habitat. It is quite possible to make a wetland area whether or not the garden already has a pond. For families with young children, a marshy area might be a safer alternative to even the shallowest pool. The marsh can be attached to the pond (see p33) or completely separate, even in a different part of the garden.

MAKING AN INDEPENDENT MARSH AREA

A natural wetland would draw its water from two sources: from above (rainwater) and from below, drawing from the underground water table. In the garden wetland, the liner is designed to retain most of the topwater and little will be drawn up from below. However, it is important to have some filtering of water through the marsh if it is not to become sour and waterlogged. Short lengths of hosepipe can be inserted through the liner into the ground below to take water out, but a few drainage holes in the bottom of the liner will do the job almost as well.

■ Choose level ground, away from overhanging trees and avoiding the main routes through the garden.

■ Dig a hollow, with gently sloping sides to a depth of between 45–60cm (18–24in). Do not make it any shallower than this as the soil will dry out too quickly in hot weather). Make a shelf around the edge, 15cm (6in) wide and 5–8cm (2–3in) deep. Remove any sharp stones.

■ Line the hollow with a flexible liner, allowing a 15cm (6in) overlap around the edge. The liner does not have to be butyl as it will be protected from sunlight by the soil – heavy duty polythene or a cheaper proprietary liner will be adequate. Secure the liner around the edge with a few heavy stones. Make a few drainage holes in the deepest part of the hollow.

■ Fill the hollow with any good, water-retentive soil. Usually the soil that has been excavated can be used, provided it has not been treated with chemicals. If it is particularly sandy, mix it with well-rotted garden compost or leaf mould. A proprietary loam-based compost can also be used.

■ Remove the anchoring stones and disguise the overlapping edge of the liner with a row of tiles, bricks or turf. Alternatively, simply cover the overlap with more soil; in time the plants will spill out from the bed and the edge will no longer be visible.

■ Wet the marsh thoroughly after construction with a hosepipe or watering can.

PLANTING UP THE MARSH

Once the marsh is completed you can start to add suitable plants. New plants should be watered in their pots before planting. Remove from their pots and, using a trowel, insert them into the damp soil, pressing them in firmly. Remember that marsh plants spread very quickly once they are established, so leave enough room for them to grow to their full size. In a small marsh it is best to leave out lady's smock, which can become invasive.

If the marsh is attached to the pond, it looks better if smaller plants are put nearest the pond, graduating the heights so that the tallest of the marsh plants are furthest away from the water. However, if the marsh is an 'island', it can be designed to be viewed from all directions. Plant tall-growing meadowsweet and hemp agrimony in the centre of the bed, using creeping plants like marsh St John's wort to spill out and disguise the edges.

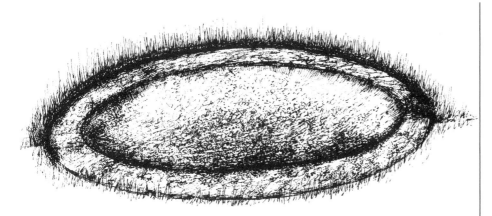

Dig a hollow with a shelf around the edge

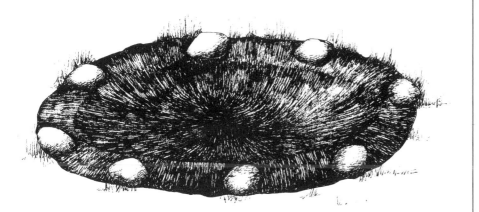

Overlap the liner around the edge and hold down with stones

The established wetland will provide a valuable additional wildlife habitat

Ragged robin

Flag iris

continued on page 48

plants
OF THE
month

SNAKESHEAD FRITILLARY
(Fritillaria meleagris)

This delicate spring flower grows naturally in the damp water meadows of southern Britain but is now very rare in the wild. It has been grown in gardens for many centuries, and makes a pretty addition to a spring-flowering meadow, grassy area or border.

type	Perennial bulb
flowers	Pink or purple with chequered markings or white with green markings, mid- to late spring
height	30cm (12in)
planting	Plant bulbs as soon as possible after purchase, in autumn. Handle carefully as they are prone to bruising. Place them 10–15cm (4–6in) deep and 15cm (6in) apart
site	Sun or light shade. In borders, meadows, or grassy areas
soil	Moist, fertile soil
care	Leave undisturbed for at least four years. Lift and divide in early summer, after leaves have died down
propagation	Once well established, snakeshead fritillary will self-seed. It can also be increased by division. Lift the bulbs in early summer, remove the offsets and replant immediately
wildlife value	Snakeshead fritillary is a useful addition to the spring meadow, providing nectar for early butterflies and insects. Moreover, like the bluebell, it is one of the most beautiful threatened wildflowers and deserves to be grown for that reason alone

Oxlip

COMMON GRAPE HYACINTH
(Muscari neglectum)

A rare wildflower in Britain, the grape hyacinth is increasingly grown in cultivation. Its natural habitat is dry grassland and it adapts well to several garden situations.

type	Perennial shrub
flowers	Deep blue, tipped with white, spring
height	20cm (8in)
planting	Plant bulbs in groups in early autumn, 8cm (3in) deep and 10cm (4in) apart
site	Open, sunny site, in grass, beds or pots
soil	Any
care	No special care needed. Clumps which are not flowering well should be lifted and divided after leaves have died back in early summer
propagation	Grape hyacinth self-seeds very readily and clumps should spread without intervention. Bulbs can also be divided and replanted in early summer
related species	Commonly grown garden species include the small, sky-blue *M. botryoides*. At only 15cm (6in) tall it is useful for rock gardens and for planting along the edges of paths
wildlife value	The strong blue colour attracts a wide range of butterflies, including tortoiseshells, brimstones and peacocks who feed on the nectar

COWSLIP

COWSLIP
(Primula veris)

One of the prettiest spring-flowering natives, the cowslip is an inhabitant of meadows and pastures. It is difficult to find in the wild, due to overpicking and to modern agricultural practices, but has become a popular garden plant.

type	Perennial
flowers	Deep yellow, orange markings in the centre, mid- to late spring
height	15–23cm (6–9in)
planting	Plant pot-grown specimens in autumn or early spring. Set the plants 23–30cm (9–12in) apart
site	Sun or partial shade, in spring-flowering meadows, grassy banks or borders
soil	Any, but dislikes acid soils
care	No special care
propagation	By division immediately after flowering or by seed collected in early summer and sown fresh. Cowslip seeds may take several years to germinate
wildlife value	An important component of the spring-flowering meadow and a vital early source of nectar for insects, particularly the spring brood of white butterflies. It is also a caterpillar food plant for the Duke of Burgundy fritillary which lays its eggs on the plant in late spring

OXLIP
(Primula elatior)
The oxlip is so closely related to the cowslip that it was not recognised as a separate species until the last century. The flowers of the oxlip are a paler yellow and do not have the orange markings. In the wild, it is most easily found in ancient coppiced woods in the east of England. It prefers a damper, shadier habitat than the cowslip and can be happily grown amongst coppiced trees, on the banks of a stream, or in a wetland habitat. Oxlips rely on early bees and butterflies for pollination.

practical project

MAKING AND
PLANTING A
WETLAND/MARSH

PLANTING TIMES
Spring is the best planting time for moisture-loving plants, but container-grown specimens will be available through to autumn from specialist nurseries.

MAINTAINING THE WETLAND

In most areas, the rainfall will be sufficient to keep the soil consistently wet. However, in times of drought, or in particularly dry areas, additional watering will be necessary. The best way to water a wetland is to allow water to trickle in gradually, either through a purpose-designed trickle irrigation system or by connecting a hosepipe to an outside tap, turned on just enough to allow water to drip out. If neither of these methods is available, check the bed regularly and top up with a watering-can as needed. As with a pond, plant foliage should be cut back in early autumn to prevent too many dead leaves clogging up the marsh. Plants which have overgrown their space can be lifted in early autumn.

WETLAND WILDLIFE

Many of the creatures attracted to a pond will also use the wetland. Frogs and toads may well spend the winter hibernating in the mud, only returning to the water to breed in the spring. Slow worms are particularly useful wetland visitors, eating large quantities of slugs and caterpillars as they nestle in the damp earth.

The flowers themselves attract pollen-eating insects, which in turn are a food source for bats and summer migrant birds like swifts and swallows and housemartins. Bees and butterflies seeking nectar will also frequent the marsh flowers. Elephant hawkmoths feed on the bogbean *(Menyanthes trifoliata)* and long-tongued hoverflies search for pollen in the flowers of lady's smock *(Cardamine pratensis)*. Lady's smock is also an important food plant for the caterpillars of orange tip butterflies.

Marsh betony *(Stachys palustris)* relies on bees for its pollination, and the heavy scent of meadowsweet *(Filipendula ulmaria)* is attractive to flies.

GROWING MARSH PLANTS IN CONTAINERS

Where space is limited, or simply as an alternative to conventional patio plants, it is possible to grow moisture-loving species in pots and tubs. The container needs to retain water – a terracotta pot which has a porous structure would not be suitable, but a glazed

PEAT BOGS

An altogether different habitat to the wetland or marsh is the peat bog, found in isolated pockets of Scotland, Wales and upland England. Peat bogs are fed by rainwater (rather than groundwater or the overflow of streams) and occur on poorly drained land. Their identifying characteristic is the sphagnum mosses which grow and decay eventually to form layers of peat. Draining these bogs to extract the peat has been one of the major threats to their continued existence. Finding alternatives to peat in the garden (such as homemade compost, leaf-mould and peat substitutes) is one of the main ways gardeners can help to safeguard natural peat bogs.

ceramic pot would work well. Plastic pots can also be used. Choose a pot at least (30cm) 12in deep and 40cm (16in) across. The best way to ensure the compost stays wet is to stand the whole pot in a substantial tray of water, so that the marsh can draw up moisture as it is needed. Ordinary plant saucers will not hold enough water, and something deeper like a large kitchen roasting tin, which may not look so elegant, will do the job more effectively.

Spring is an ideal time to plant moisture-loving plants. Fill the container with a loam-based potting compost, insert the plants and water until soaked. Choose plants that won't outgrow the limited space too quickly. Include a selection of tall-growing species like purple loosestrife *(Lythrum salicaria)*, sweet flag *(Acorus calamus)* and ragged robin *(Lychnis flos-cuculi)* alongside smaller plants like bogbean *(Menyanthes trifoliata)* and oxlips *(Primula elatior)*. Avoid lady's smock *(Cardamine pratensis)* and water mint *(Mentha aquatica)* which can spread too quickly.

Keep the water in the base tray topped up, using rainwater collected in a water butt where possible. Keeping the tray full of water is particularly important in long, hot, dry spells, although in spring and autumn the natural rainfall will probably be adequate. Cut back the foliage in the autumn to prevent the pots becoming choked with decaying material. Repot the plants every two or three years when they start to outgrow their containers. In the second year after planting, the plants may have used up the nutrients in the compost and will need an extra boost from a slow-release fertiliser.

MOISTURE-LOVING NATIVE PLANTS

plant	height	colour	flowering time
BOG BEAN *(Menyanthes trifoliata)* **M**	25cm (10in)	White	Mid-summer
GLOBE FLOWER *(Trollius europaeus)*	60cm (24in)	Yellow	Early summer
OXLIP *(Primula elatior)* **B, N**	15cm (6in)	Pale yellow	Late spring
PRIMROSE *(Primula vulgaris)* **N**	10cm (4in)	Pale yellow	Mid-spring
PURPLE LOOSESTRIFE *(Lythrum salicaria)* **B, N**	1m (3ft)	Pink-purple	Summer
RAGGED ROBIN *(Lychnis flos-cuculi)* **N**	60cm (24in)	Pink	Summer
SWEET FLAG *(Acorus calamus)*	60cm (24in)	Green	Mid-summer
BOG ARUM* *(Calla palustris)*	15cm (6in)	Yellow-green	Summer
HEMP AGRIMONY *(Eupatorium cannabinum)* **B, N**	4ft (1.2m)	Reddish-pink	Late summer
LADY'S SMOCK *(Cardamine pratensis)* **H, C, N**	23cm (9in)	Pale pink	Spring
MARSH BETONY *(Stachys palustris)* **B**	30cm (12in)	Purple	Summer
MARSH CINQUEFOIL *(Potentilla palustris)*	23cm (9in)	Dark red	Summer
MARSH ST JOHN'S WORT *(Hypericum elodes)*	15cm (6in)	Pale yellow	Summer
MEADOWSWEET *(Filipendula ulmaria)*	1m (3ft)	Creamy-white	Summer

* Naturalised in places in Britain

M A Y

The coming of the hawthorn blossom is one of the most reliable
signs of spring. Lanes and hedgerows are filled with the distinctive
scent and this is a good time to consider which native shrubs and
trees could be used in the garden. Wild cherry is another tree at its
best this month, the blossom swarming with insects as they forage
from flower to flower in search of nectar and pollen.

Visiting old woodlands can be a source of inspiration for the
wildlife gardener. Carpets of bluebells still exist in traditionally
managed sites, where trampling by hoards of visitors is kept to a
minimum. The cycle of coppicing trees in winter to regrow during
the summer suits the bluebell perfectly. The woodland is opened up
to the sunlight while the foliage and flowers are forming, but
reverts to shade during the hotter summer months. Bluebells are
very resistant to change and in some areas the plants persist,
despite the fact that the original woodland has disappeared. In
towns, evidence of lost bluebell woods may surface in street names
like 'Endymion', or perhaps in the memories of the oldest
residents.

Two garden 'friends' are worth observing this month. Hedgehogs
are particularly active, finding partners for mating, and feeding
voraciously at night. Unfortunately many hedgehogs are killed due
to lack of forethought on the gardeners' part, either by getting
caught in badly placed netting, eating slugs which have been
poisoned by pellets, or by drowning in steep-sided ponds. Another
useful garden inhabitant is the lacewing which lays its eggs on a
variety of plant leaves. The brown larvae that hatch out feed
greedily on aphids and small caterpillars, to grow into delicate
green-coloured adults.

tasks

FOR THE

month

AVOID PLANTING IN THE HEAT
If weather is warm, do planting in the late afternoon or evening to prevent plants from wilting in the heat.

CHECKLIST

- ☐ Plant out half-hardy annuals
- ☐ Clear spring borders
- ☐ Lift and divide primroses
- ☐ Prune flowering currant bushes
- ☐ Planting hanging baskets
- ☐ Plant for summer and autumn

PLANTING OUT HALF-HARDY ANNUALS

In most areas, it will be safe to plant out half-hardy annuals like *Nicotiana* after the danger of frost is past. These may have been raised from seed indoors or in a greenhouse (see p29) or they can be bought this month from garden centres and markets as bedding plants. Although growing half-hardy species involves more work than perennials and hardy annuals, they will provide an extra source of pollen and nectar throughout the summer.

Preparation

Use small plants or seedlings to fill up gaps in existing beds, or to plant up containers and hanging baskets. Garden beds should be prepared by forking over the top 15–20cm (6–8in) to break up the soil to a fine texture. Fill containers with proprietary potting compost. The soil or compost should be moist before planting, so water thoroughly the day before planting if necessary. All half-hardy annuals prefer an open, sunny position.

Planting

- Separate each plant, making sure that there is a healthy root system.

- Space the plants about half their eventual height apart. Make planting holes with a trowel and firm each plant into place.

NOTE

- *Watering should not be necessary, unless there are prolonged periods without rain* ▪

CLEAR SPRING BORDERS

Borders or pots containing spring-flowering biennials (like wallflowers and forget-me-nots which will be reaching the end of their flowering period) can be cleared to make room for sowing hardy annual seeds (see p40) or for half-hardy bedding plants (see earlier). This will ensure there is a good range of nectar-producing plants in flower throughout the summer. Pull up the biennials and add to the compost heap. Fork over the soil, ready for replanting.

LIFT AND DIVIDE PRIMROSES

Wild primroses (*Primula vulgaris*) and any garden primroses or polyanthus can be divided this month, after flowering has finished. This is a simple way of thinning out overcrowded clumps and increasing the number of plants available.

- Ease the clumps gently out of the ground with a hand fork, taking care not to tear the roots.

- Select pieces with a few roots attached and pull apart by hand. Pot them up into moist potting compost and place the pots in a shady corner of the garden.

- Keep moist throughout the summer and plant out into their permanent positions in early autumn.

PRUNING FLOWERING CURRANT

Flowering currant shrubs (*Ribes*) may be pruned if the plant has become too large.

■ Wait until flowering has finished. Cut out the old, woody stems near the base of the plant, making the cut just above a new bud.

■ Removing most of the old wood will thin out the plant considerably.

■ Young stems should then be shortened by about a third, making the cut at the junction with a strong shoot lower down.

PLANTING HANGING BASKETS

It is possible to provide instant nectar for the summer months by planting up a hanging basket. Half-hardy and hardy annuals are widely available in garden centres – choose from varieties like alyssum or nasturtiums, mixed with upright French marigolds, petunias or snapdragons.

> ### NOTE
> ■ *Stand the basket on an upturned bucket while planting* ■

■ Use a solid plastic or terracotta hanging basket.

■ Cover the base with a 5cm (2in) layer of coarse grit.

■ Add 8cm (3in) of potting compost.

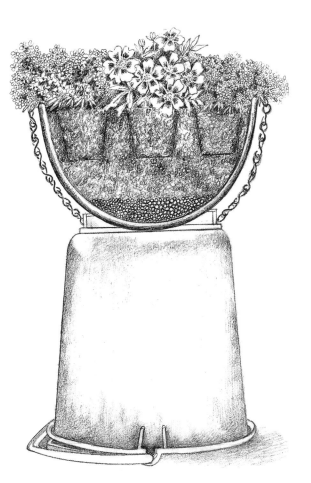

■ Arrange the plants so that the trailing varieties are at the edge and the upright ones in the centre.

■ Fill around the plants with more compost until it is just below the rim of the basket. Firm the plants in well.

■ Water thoroughly.

Alternative hanging basket
Instead of the traditional flowers, plant up a basket of herbs. Even a simple combination of mint and chives will attract bees, butterflies and moths. For visual effect, use several different types of mint, including the variegated varieties. Allow the chives and mints to flower for maximum wildlife value.

PLANTING FOR SUMMER AND AUTUMN

Buying bulbs and pot-grown plants means you can stock up the garden, even if you have grown nothing from seed. Ornamental onions (alliums) are available as bulbs and may still flower in late summer if put in early this month – if not, they will certainly be well established for next year. Autumn-flowering cyclamen tubers (*Cyclamen hederifolium*) can also be planted for flowering in late summer and autumn.

plants

OF THE

month

RAMSONS/WILD GARLIC
(Allium ursinum)

A native bulb of hedgerows, coppiced woods and shady banks, ramsons is increasingly available from wildflower nurseries. It is one of the most common members of the onion family and the leaves give off a powerful garlic smell when crushed.

type	Bulb
flowers	White, mid-spring to early summer
height	40cm (16in)
planting	Plant bulbs in early autumn at twice their own depth
site	Partial shade, in a coppiced wood, under deciduous trees or hedges
soil	Moist
care	Once established, clumps may be divided after flowering to produce more plants
propagation	Lift and divide bulbs in summer (after flowering), replanting the offsets and small bulbs immediately. Ramsons also self-seeds very readily
related species	Most of the ornamental onions (alliums) are good for bees and butterflies, with their large pom-pom flowers – in particular, *A. sphaerocephalon, A. giganteum* and *A. aflatunense*
wildlife value	Although not rare in the wild, ramsons is a good plant to grow alongside more precious woodland flowers such as bluebells. Attractive to butterflies, wasps and flying insects

GARDEN ALLIUMS
The summer-flowering alliums are easy to grow and worth a special place in the wildlife garden. Unlike the wild garlic, they need a sunny spot and a well-drained soil. Allium sphaerocephalon has rounded heads of dark red flowers which are irresistible to tortoiseshell butterflies. The striking Allium giganteum growing to 4ft (1.2m) or more is hard to ignore; the purple flowerheads act as a magnet to bees, butterflies and flying insects. Plant the bulbs in early autumn for flowers in early summer.

RAMSONS/WILD GARLIC

practical project

PLANTING A NATIVE HEDGE

Hedges have been an integral part of the cultivated landscape in Britain since at least Anglo-Saxon times and probably since the Bronze Age. Different types of hedges were planted for different purposes: a double hedge, for example, would mark an important boundary whilst a hedge designed to contain livestock would be particularly impenetrable at the base. Almost incidentally they became shelters and pathways for wildlife, harbouring birds, mammals and insects. In the garden, a hedge of native species can serve both as a wildlife provider and as an effective division between neighbouring plots.

CHOOSING THE SPECIES

Monoculture – the planting of only one species in a hedge – is accepted gardening practice. Native species like yew, beech, holly and hawthorn have traditionally been used to make garden boundaries and although they make indisputably fine hedges,

their use as a wildlife corridor is limited. A mixed hedge, on the other hand, provides a much wider resource and a greater number of animal and flower species will soon become associated with it. A balanced hedge might include a large proportion of one of the mainstay species such as hawthorn, which forms a dense, thorny structure, as well as blossoms and berries. This may be interspersed with four or five other species which flower and fruit at different times, and should include at least one evergreen to provide shelter in winter.

HOW TO PLANT A HEDGE

■ Choose two-year-old seedlings, which are large enough to handle, but should not need staking.

■ Mark out the length of the hedge with canes and string. It does not have to be a straight line, a curving hedge works just as well.

TREES/SHRUBS SUITABLE FOR HEDGING

plant	description	plant	description
ALDER BUCKTHORN		**FIELD MAPLE**	
(*Frangula alnus*)	Deciduous, fruit	(*Acer campestre*)	Deciduous, autumn colour
BEECH		**HAWTHORN**	
(*Fagus sylvatica*)	Slow-growing, deciduous, autumn colour	(*Crataegus monogyna*)	Deciduous, blossom, berries
BLACKTHORN		**HAZEL**	
(*Prunus spinosa*)	Deciduous, blossom, fruit	(*Corylus avellana*)	Deciduous, catkins, nuts
CRAB APPLE		**HOLLY**	
(*Malus sylvestris*)	Deciduous, blossom, fruit	(*Ilex aquifolium*)	Slow-growing, evergreen, berries
DOG ROSE		**WILD PRIVET**	
(*Rosa canina*)	Deciduous, blossom, hips	(*Ligustrum ovalifolium*)	Quick-growing, evergreen
ELM		**YEW**	
(*Ulmus procera*)	Deciduous	(*Taxus baccata*)	Slow-growing, evergreen

PLANTING TIMES
Container-grown hedging plants can be planted at any time during the year, except when the ground is baked hard or frozen. However, the best time for planting evergreens is late spring and the best time for deciduous species is late autumn. Bare-root plants should only be put in when they are dormant, between late autumn and early spring.

Dig a trench 60cm (2ft) wide and 45cm (18in) deep

Set the plants 30–45cm (12–18in) apart in the trench

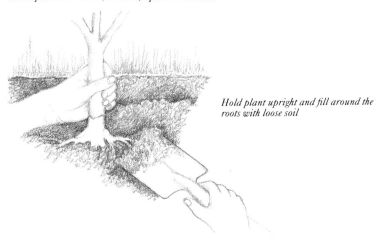

Hold plant upright and fill around the roots with loose soil

WILDLIFE USES FOR HEDGING

Caterpillars of brimstone butterflies feed on alder buckthorn

Blackthorn, hawthorn, hazel and privet provide nectar for many species of butterfly

Thrushes, dunnocks, garden warblers and finches use the hedgerow for nesting

Hedgehogs, voles and woodmice shelter and feed in the hedge bottom

Hawthorn, blackthorn and holly provide berries for birds in winter

■ Dig a trench in front of the line, 60cm (2ft) wide and 45cm (18in) deep, running the entire length of the proposed hedge. Remove weed roots and large stones whilst digging.

■ Add a layer of organic matter (garden compost or well-rotted manure) and mix with the loose soil at the bottom of the trench.

■ Set the plants, 30–45cm (12–18in) apart and at the same depth as they were in the nursery (shown by the soil mark on the stem), adding more soil to the bottom of the trench, if necessary, to ensure the plant will sit at the right depth.

■ Holding the plant upright, fill around the roots with loose soil, until it reaches the soil mark, firming down well.

IMMEDIATE AFTERCARE

Water the new plants thoroughly, making sure the water soaks down around the roots. Cut back the top and side growths by at least one third – this will encourage side branching and bushy growth.

continued on page 60

plants
OF THE
month

LILY OF THE VALLEY
(Convallaria majalis)

A relatively rare native plant of woodlands and meadows. It is widely grown in gardens for its sweet scent and nodding bell-like flowers, but needs a shady corner to establish well.

type	Rhizome
flowers	White, late spring/early summer
fruits	Small red berries, late summer
height	15–20cm (6–8in)
spread	60cm (24in)
planting	Plant crowns 8cm (3in) apart, singly or in groups, in early autumn
site	Full or partial shade, under deciduous trees, in shrub borders or woodland
soil	Prefers a soil containing leaf mould which will retain moisture and prevent the roots from drying out
care	Mulch around the plants in spring with leaf mould or garden compost. Lift and divide overgrown clumps in autumn or late winter, if necessary
propagation	Lily of the valley spreads naturally by its underground rhizomes. New plants can be made by dividing and replanting the crowns in autumn or late winter
wildlife value	An increasingly uncommon plant in the wild, it is a useful component of a woodland habitat

BROOM
(Cytisus scoparius)

A common native shrub of dry, sunny habitats, broom was traditionally grown for its bark, used in the tanning industry and for making ropes. The long-lasting golden yellow flowers make it a useful wildlife garden plant.

type	Deciduous shrub
flowers	Yellow, late spring/early summer
height	2.5m (8ft)
spread	2.5m (8ft)
planting	Plant container-grown specimens in autumn or early spring
site	Full sun, shrub border
soil	Any, well-drained
care	Prune each year to prevent shrub becoming bare and leggy. In mid-summer, cut back only the stems that have just flowered. Take care not to cut into old wood as this will stop any new growth Brooms tend to be short-lived and old bushes do not respond to pruning, so should be discarded after six or seven years
propagation	Take hardwood cuttings in late summer
related species	*C.* × *praecox* is a more compact bush for the smaller garden, growing to 1.5m (5ft). It flowers a month earlier
wildlife value	The yellow flowers last for up to two months and are excellent pollen providers for bees

WILD CHERRY
(Prunus avium)

Sometimes known by its older name of 'gean', the wild cherry forms a spreading tree which is only really suited to the largest gardens. It is the parent of most of the fruiting and ornamental cherries in cultivation and is grown not only for its flowers and fruit but also for the crimson colour of the leaves in autumn.

type	Deciduous tree
flowers	White, mid- to late spring
fruits	Yellow, red or black berries, sweet or bitter, late summer
height	18m (60ft)
spread	6–8m (20–25ft)
planting	Plant young trees, 1–2m (3–6½ft) high, between late autumn and early spring, when the ground is workable
site	In woodland or as an individual specimen tree. Plant at least 27m (90ft) away from the nearest building
soil	Fertile, well-drained soil preferred, but will tolerate most ordinary garden soils
care	No regular pruning required
propagation	In the wild, the cherry spreads by throwing up suckers from its base, which are clones of the parent plant. Occasionally the stones are planted by birds and may germinate some way away from the parent tree. In the garden, propagation is by seed. Sow cherry stones outdoors in pots as soon as the fruit is ripe and allow the cold weather to encourage germination
varieties	*P. avium* 'Plena' is one of the most popular cultivars, growing to a height of 12m (40ft). It has masses of double white flowers, but the fruits are rarely set
wildlife value	Wild cherry depends on bees and hoverflies working the flowers for its pollination. The flowers also attract several species of butterfly, particularly peacocks. It supports a range of native beetles and the fruit is popular with birds

BIRD CHERRY
(Prunus padus)

A smaller relative of the wild cherry, this tree got its common name quite possibly because of the fruit which, although bitter to human taste, is eaten by birds. A common native of woods and hedgerows.

type	Deciduous tree or shrub
flowers	White, late spring
fruits	Black cherries, bitter, late summer
height	15m (50ft)
spread	5–6m (15–20ft)
planting	Plant young trees, 1–2m (3–6½ft) high, between autumn and early spring, when the weather allows
site	In woodland or shrub borders
soil	Any well drained
care	No pruning required
propagation	By seed taken from the ripened fruit (see wild cherry)
varieties	The most common cultivated variety is 'Watereri' which has longer, drooping flowerheads
wildlife value	Heavily scented racemes of blossom invite a number of flying insects. The fruit is quickly picked off by the birds, particularly blackbirds

DWARF CHERRY
If space is limited there is a native dwarf cherry (Prunus cerasus) which will serve the wildlife equally well. As a shrub it grows no higher than 5m (15ft) and can be incorporated in hedges or a shrub border. It bears pinkish-white flowers and has acid-tasting red berries.

practical project

PLANTING A NATIVE HEDGE

MAINTENANCE

Each spring, whilst the hedge is still forming, prune the top and side shoots by one third. Do not leave the central stem to grow to the desired height of the hedge before cutting back. Regular pruning will ensure that by the time the hedge does reach its final height, it will have developed a strong, dense framework.

It is a good idea to apply a mulch of garden compost, leaf mould or chopped bark around the plants each spring. This will discourage weeds (which may strangle the young hedge) and form a good environment for hedgerow plants and microscopic creatures.

CLIPPING

The main difference between conventional hedge care and those managed for wildlife is in the clipping. Wildlife hedges should never be clipped before nesting is completely finished; usually it is safe to do so in late summer or early autumn, but if in doubt, leave until the winter. (For details on hedge trimming see p89.)

WILDLIFE TO EXPECT

Blackbirds, thrushes, dunnocks, sparrows, greenfinches and bullfinches all prefer the dense, protected growth of a hedge to any other nesting site. They will be joined in the summer by shy, ground-feeding wrens, who search the leaf litter beneath the hedge for spiders and other insects. Many other garden birds like tits and robins will use the hedge simply as a convenient perch, for picking off caterpillars from the leafy growth. The hedge foliage is a particularly good breeding ground for moths such as the privet hawkmoth, garden spiders who leave their mark in the shape of finely woven webs and the often heard, but rarely seen, bush cricket. At ground level, the wildlife residents are most likely to be hedgehogs, wood mice and bank voles, although toads and frogs often hide in the shelter of a hedge bottom. In time a native hedge will become a busy wildlife corridor offering shelter, food and a convenient route from one part of the garden to another.

HEDGEROW FLOWERS

Although the soil at the base of the hedge may be poor, a surprising number of wildflowers seem to thrive there. The orientation of the hedge will determine which flowers may be grown. South-facing hedges receive a good deal of sun whilst north faces may be in almost complete shade. Choose a selection of plants to suit the position of your hedge.

Most of the hedgerow flowers tolerate a dry, poor soil, but one or two such as primroses and lesser celandines need to be kept moist. Unless the hedge is by a stream or pool, it is unlikely that their needs will be met; they would be happier in a damp ditch or marshy area.

Pot-grown plants can be planted out any time from spring to autumn. In the first two years of the hedge's growth, avoid putting in the taller plants, such as sweet cicely, which may compete with the new hedging. It is also advisable to wait until the hedge is well-established (five years or more) before putting in hedgerow climbers, like traveller's joy *(Clematis vitalba)*. Its scrambling habit is ideal for dense, well-grown hedges, but it can easily strangle younger plants.

It is best to use small, healthy plants for the hedge bottom and not seedlings, whose roots may not be sufficiently developed to cope with the poor soil. Insert the new plants with a trowel and water thoroughly. Water regularly for the first two weeks – particularly if there is a hot, dry spell.

ANCIENT HEDGEROWS

We often hear and read of 'ancient hedgerows', but just how old are the hedges we see in the countryside today? The Anglo-Saxons certainly planted mixed hedgerows which incorporated naturally growing trees and shrubs as well as specially planted ones. However, most of the hedges we see today were laid out between 1750 and 1850 – the so-called 'Enclosure' years, when large open areas were enclosed to make the smaller, rectangular fields we know today – involving the planting of some 200,000 miles of hedging. The earlier hedges contained a wide range of species, but for economic reasons enclosure hedges were normally one species only – usually hawthorn (Crataegus monogyna).

RECOMMENDED NATIVE HEDGEROW FLOWERS

plant	type	position	soil	wildlife value
BETONY *(Stachys officinalis)*	Perennial	Sun or shade	Any	Bees, butterflies
BLUEBELL *(Scilla non-scripta)*	Bulb	Sun or shade	Any	Bees, butterflies
COMMON DOG VIOLET *(Viola riviana)*	Perennial	Partial shade	Any	Caterpillar food plant for fritillary butterflies
GARLIC MUSTARD *(Alliaria petiolata)*	Biennial	Partial shade	Any	Caterpillar food plant for orange tips, tortoiseshells and whites
GREATER STICHWORT *(Stellaria holostea)*	Perennial	Partial shade	Any	Bees, moths, butterflies
HEDGE WOUNDWORT *(Stachys sylvatica)*	Perennial	Partial shade	Any	Bees, butterflies
HEDGEROW CRANESBILL *(Geranium pyrenaicum)*	Perennial	Partial shade	Any	
LESSER CELANDINE *(Ranunculus ficaria)*	Perennial	Partial shade	Damp	Bees, butterflies
PRIMROSE *(Primula vulgaris)*	Perennial	Sun or shade	Damp	Butterflies (whites)
RED CAMPION *(Silene Dioca)*	Perennial	Sun or shade	Any	Butterflies
SELFHEAL *(Prunella vulgaris)*	Perennial	Sun or shade	Any	Bees, butterflies
SWEET CICELY *(Myrrhis odorata)*	Perennial	Sun or shade	Any	Bees
WHITE DEADNETTLE *(Lamium maculatum album)*	Perennial	Sun or shade	Any	Bees

M A Y

JUNE

By early summer most of the garden's wildlife are busy bringing up their young. In the pond, tadpoles are turning into adults and are at their most vulnerable as they emerge from the water and seek shelter from predators amongst the marginal plants. Resident garden birds like blackbirds are starting their second brood, although newly arrived migrants like the garden warblers have yet to mate. Bats produce their single offspring this month and the adults can be seen swooping around the house and garden at dusk to feed.

Young hedgehogs are also being born now in litters of four or five. Although born blind, within two weeks their eyes will be open and the brown adult spines starting to develop. The parents feed at night and can often be heard shuffling around the garden in the darkness. This is the best time to watch for fox cubs, as they leave the safety of the earth to explore their immediate surroundings.

A healthy garden pond will be home to large numbers of dragonflies and damselflies. There are around forty different species in Britain and their spectacular wings and dazzling colours make good viewing. Often, the only way to tell the difference between the two insects is to watch them in flight – the gentle flutter of the damselfly in contrast to the dragonfly's powerful darting movements. The aerial acrobatic displays denote mating, and before long eggs will be laid just under the water, frequently on the stems of aquatic plants.

For traditional gardeners, summer means roses. In the wildlife garden, too, many of the native shrub roses come in to flower. They demand far less attention than their hybrid counterparts and are equally effective in providing nectar and hips for insects and birds.

tasks

FOR THE

month

C H E C K L I S T

- Feed hedgehogs
- Lift and divide spring-flowering bulbs
- Clear pond of algae and pondweed
- Cut down the nettle patch
- Sow biennial seeds outdoors
- Cut spring-flowering meadow
- Divide irises

PROVIDING EXTRA FOOD FOR HEDGEHOGS

In dry spells, when slugs, snails and worms may not be so easy to come by, garden hedgehogs can be given an artificial diet boost. This is particularly important now, when the babies are being born and the females are suckling and unable to travel far for food. Put out a saucer of tinned pet food and one of water each night in a regular spot. Don't feed bread and milk which upsets the hedgehog's digestive system.

LIFTING AND DIVIDING BULBS

When the spring bulbs have finished flowering and the leaves have begun to die back, they can be lifted to increase the number of plants. Choose clumps that have been undisturbed for at least three years; a poor show of flowers indicates that the bulbs are becoming congested underground. This method is applicable to grape hyacinths, bluebells, snakeshead fritillary, ramsons garlic, daffodils, crocuses and tulips.

■ Insert a fork well clear of

the clump and push it down deeply to come up under the bulbs. Gently ease the complete clump out of the ground. Remove the excess soil and discard any bulbs which are soft or rotten. Detach the small bulbs and the bulbils for replanting.

■ Replant the large bulbs immediately at normal planting depth (see p108). The small bulbs should also be planted straight away at two thirds of their usual planting depth. The tiny bulbils only need to be covered with their own depth of soil. Small bulbs will not flower in their first year and bulbils may take up to four years to reach maturity, so it is a good idea to put them into a separate nursery bed.

■ Alternatively, they can be planted directly amongst the existing bulbs, where they will eventually create

a denser display, but remember to allow enough room for each bulb to develop to its full size.

CLEARING POND OF ALGAE AND PONDWEED

Warm weather leads to a growth of pondweed and algae, which can choke the pond if not checked. Don't be tempted to use chemicals which will indiscriminately kill the water creatures. Rake the excess growth out with a garden rake, and lay it by the side of the pond for a day or so. This allows at least some of the insects and water snails to find their way back to the water. Then add the vegetation to the compost heap.

CUTTING DOWN THE NETTLE PATCH

If a small part of the garden has been developed as a stinging nettle patch (see p81), cut down half of the plants now to provide new growth for the next generation of butterflies. Small tortoiseshells, peacocks, commas and red admirals will lay their eggs on the shoots to make sure that the emerging caterpillars are well supplied with a diet of young nettle leaves.

SOWING SEEDS OF BIENNIALS

Many useful flowering plants can be started off now from seed for flowering next year. Biennials sown now and planted out in the autumn will flower next spring or summer, for one year only.

Sowing biennials

Biennial seeds may be sown either in pots or, if there is room, in nursery beds in the garden. Pots should be filled with seed compost and the soil in the bed raked to a fine texture. Both soil and compost should be moist before sowing. Choose a lightly shaded position to protect the new seedlings from the heat of the summer sun.

■ Sow the seeds, thinly spaced and about 1cm (½in) deep. In beds this can be done by sprinkling the seed and then raking lightly to ensure that the seed lies just beneath the surface of the soil. In pots, seeds can be pressed lightly into the compost by hand.

■ Water well, using a watering-can fitted with a fine sprinkler rose. Remember to mark the positions of the different species.

Aftercare

Six weeks after sowing, crowded seedlings should be thinned out and transplanted to additional

pots or beds. Young plants must never be allowed to dry out. In mid-summer, pinch out the tip of each plant to encourage bushy growth. Plant out the grown plants in mid-autumn to their permanent flowering positions.

●

CUTTING THE SPRING-FLOWERING MEADOW

Established wildflower lawns or meadows which have been managed specifically for spring-flowering plants like cowslips and fritillaries can be cut once they have finished. This is at the expense of summer-flowering species but enables the grass to be used as a conventional lawn for the rest of the season.

Use a sturdy rotary mower, hand or motor-scythe and cut back to 10cm (4in) high. Leave the cuttings on the grass for a day or so, to allow insects and seeds time to find their way back to ground. Rake off and add the clippings (sparingly) to the compost heap or use as a mulch around shrubs and perennials to suppress weeds and conserve moisture.

WARNING

■ *Hand and motor-scythes can be dangerous if not handled properly. If in doubt, get professional help* ■

●

DIVIDING IRISES

Bearded garden irises *(Iris*

germanica) and the native yellow flag iris *(Iris pseudacorus)* can be lifted and divided now if they have become overcrowded.

■ After flowering, lift the clumps out of the soil with a fork.

■ Select healthy young pieces of rhizome and cut them away from the main clump with a knife. Discard the older parts from the centre.

■ Cut back the leaves to 23cm (9in) to make them more stable in the wind.

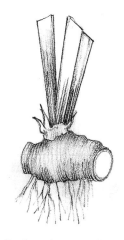

■ Replant the new pieces so that the rhizome just shows above the soil.

■ Ensure newly-planted rhizomes have an adequate supply of water until their roots have re-established themselves.

BIENNIALS

Evening primrose
(Oenothera biennis) B, M, H
Flowers – early summer to mid-autumn

Forget-me-not
(Myosotis sylvatica) N, B, Nat
Flowers – mid-spring to mid-summer

Foxglove
(Digitalis purpurea) B, Po, Nat
Flowers – early to mid-summer

Great mullein
(Verbascum thapsus) B, Nat
Flowers – summer

Honesty *(Lunaria biennis)* N, S
Flowers – mid-spring to early summer

Sweet rocket
(Hesperis matronalis) N, Nat
Flowers – early summer

Sweet william
(Dianthus barbatus) N
Flowers – early summer

Teasel
(Dipsacus fullonum) N, B, S, Nat
Flowers – late summer

Wallflower
(Cheiranthus cheiri) N, Nat
Flowers – late spring

plants
OF THE
month

HONEYSUCKLE
(Lonicera periclymenum)

Also known as woodbine, the native honeysuckle is frequently seen scrambling through
hedgerows or growing amongst shrubs in open
woodlands. In old oak woods, the summer-
visiting pied flycatcher relies almost exclusively on honeysuckle bark for nest building.
As these woods are destroyed or left un-
coppiced, honeysuckle declines and these rare
birds have fewer and fewer places to breed.

type	Deciduous climber
flowers	Creamy white, tinged with purple, summer
fruits	Red berries, autumn
height	To 6m (20ft)
habit	Scrambling, twining stems
planting	Plant in autumn or early spring
site	Sun or light shade. Ideally with the roots in shade and the top in sun. Against a wall, fence or trellis, over an arch or pergola, through a hedge or old tree
soil	Any, well-drained soil
care	No special care needed. A mulch of well-rotted manure or compost can be put around the roots in spring, but is not essential. Regular pruning is not required. Remove old wood from overgrown specimens after flowering
propagation	Hardwood cuttings taken in early to mid-autumn. Seed can also be collected from ripe berries
varieties	Several garden varieties are useful for their fragrance, nectar and berries, particularly the early-flowering *L. periclymenum* 'Belgica' and the late-flowering *L. periclymenum* 'Serotina' (Dutch honeysuckles), which can extend the flowering season from late spring to mid-autumn. There are also two winter-flowering species, *L. fragrantissima* and *L. standishii*
wildlife value	The strong night-time scent is particularly attractive to hawk-moths seeking nectar. During the day, only long-tongued bumble bees can reach the nectar in the trumpet-shaped flowers. In spring, the new shoots are popular with blackfly, but these in turn provide food for ladybirds, lacewings and the new brood of baby birds. Strips of honeysuckle bark are taken by sparrows and blackbirds for nest building and visiting pied flycatchers. A dense tangle of honeysuckle stems against a wall may prove a successful nesting site. In autumn the berries are eaten by birds, although they are poisonous to humans

DUTCH HONEYSUCKLE

ROSES FOR A WILDLIFE GARDEN

Roses tend to be used as specimen plants, grown in isolated beds for their prize blooms, and seem to be of little relevance to the wildlife gardener. Yet several of the species and wild roses are really useful in the wildlife garden, as part of the underlayer in the woodland, as hedges, or as part of a conventional shrub border. Shrub roses are versatile and the blooms are just as pleasing (if somewhat smaller) than the hybrid teas and floribundas. The simple flowers provide easily accessible pollen for bumble bees and hoverflies, plus colourful hips for birds, foxes and wood mice in the autumn. Even the leaves have a use for one type of bee, the female leaf-cutter, who cuts out semi-circular pieces of leaf to line her nest.

FIELD ROSE

WILD AND SPECIES SHRUB ROSES

Rosa rugosa

Introduced from China, but widely naturalised in Britain and Europe. Heavily scented blooms.

flowers	Deep pink, mid- to late summer
flower size	4–8cm (1½–3in), solitary
hips	Large, orange-red, early autumn
height	1.8m (6ft)
spread	1.2m (4ft)
uses	Hedging, shrub borders

DOG ROSE *Rosa canina*

The most common native rose, found growing wild in hedgerows and on roadsides.

flowers	Pale pink or white, mid-summer
flower size	5cm (2in), in clusters
hips	Red, autumn
height	2.5m (8ft)
spread	1.8m (6ft)
uses	Hedging, woodland edge

Rosa glauca (syn. *R. rubrifolia*)

Native to central and southern Europe, but widely grown in British gardens for its purple-grey foliage, dark stems and abundant hips. Look out for self-sown seedlings.

flowers	Purplish-pink, mid-summer
flower size	4cm (1½in), in clusters
hips	Reddish-brown when ripe, autumn
height	2.2m (7ft)
spread	1.5m (5ft)
uses	Woodland edge, shrub border

SWEET BRIAR *Rosa rubiginosa*

Another native wild rose of scrub and grass banks. Leaves have a strong apple scent when crushed.

flowers	Bright pink, in small clusters, mid-summer
flower size	2.5cm (1in)
hips	Bright red, autumn
height	2.5m (8ft)
spread	2.5m (8ft)
uses	Hedging, shrub borders, woodland edge

CULTIVATION
of wild and species shrub roses

site	Sun or light shade
soil	Any, well-drained soil
planting	Plant new bushes between late autumn and early spring, when the ground is not too hard. Add garden compost of well-rotted manure to the planting hole. Set hedging plants 30–45cm (12–18in) apart
care	No regular pruning needed, but untidy bushes or hedges can be trimmed in late winter. Take out weak stems at ground level and remove straggly growing tips. Mulch in spring with grass clippings, garden compost or leaf mould
propagation	From cuttings taken in late summer/early autumn

FIELD ROSE
(Rosa arvensis)
Found growing in the hedgerows and woodlands at the margins of fields rather than in the fields themselves. It is a widespread native rose in Britain, bearing solitary white flowers throughout the summer.

practical project

PLANTING WALLS AND ROCK BANKS

In natural conditions, a dry, rocky landscape hosts a diverse collection of plants and animals which are specific to this terrain. Very few gardens incorporate a cliff or mountain slope but it is possible to recreate these habitats on a smaller scale, particularly if the garden already includes an old wall, or rockery. Even paths and paving stones can be interplanted with species that prefer a shallow soil and new walls can be adapted to 'take' new species.

There are several good reasons for incorporating this kind of specialised habitat into a wildlife garden. Many of the native rock plants are becoming rare in the countryside and the garden can play an important conservation role. The habitat will also greatly increase the range of wildlife that use the garden, some of which will only be attracted to the dry conditions and specialised plants that grow here. Rock plants are amongst some of the prettiest species and deserve to be grown for that reason alone.

WALL PLANTING

Old brick or stone walls are excellent wildlife 'centres'. Plants root and flourish in the soft lime mortar just as they would in the crevices of limestone rocks in the wild. New walls, held together with cement rather than mortar, tend to have less plant growth, but with time and weathering the cement will soften and allow seedlings to get a hold and grow on.

Even without planting, older walls may host a range of mosses, various types of lichen and, where the air is moist, ferns like wall rue and the maidenhair spleenwort. Larger plants like elder and buddleia are often found clinging precariously high on town walls, their seeds having been deposited there by birds.

A good wall creates its own microclimate, usually warmer than the surrounding garden, where wall butterflies and hawkmoths will bask in the reflected warmth. Spiders and beetles use the crevices to keep cool and solitary mason bees and wasps make chambers in the mortar. A wall top is often used by birds as a boundary to their territory; blackbirds and robins are particularly territorial and will sit on top of the wall to warn off their rivals with noisy displays of aggression. Old walls, with loose bricks may house hole-nesting wrens, robins, great tits, redstarts or spotted flycatchers.

Planting in a wall

The best walls are low and loosely constructed with plenty of gaps and pockets for planting. Most plants prefer some soil, however poor or shallow, and this can be added where necessary. It is best to put in young plants in spring or autumn and water well until established. If the crevices between the stones are very small, individual seeds or seedlings can be planted instead. In time, the plants will self-seed and spread.

Flowering wall plants are listed in the table on page 72.

CONSTRUCTING A ROCK BANK

If the garden has no manmade rockery or natural outcrops of rock for planting, it is possible to make a rock bank to provide a useful wildlife habitat. This is a simple construction and far less costly than a full-scale rock garden.

■ Stack stones randomly to form a double-sided wall to the desired height and length.

■ Between each layer of stones, add a mixture of stone chippings or gravel and loam potting compost (this makes a good growing medium for rock plants, but if not available any poor, stony garden soil can be substituted).

■ Leave some gaps between the stones without any soil, to allow access to the interior for small mammals and creatures.

■ Lay more stones or rocks across the top of the structure to form a 'lid'. The planting pockets can then be planted with any of the rock or wall plants listed opposite and on page 72.

RECOMMENDED PLANTS FOR ROCK BANKS AND GARDENS

plant	flower	height	wildlife value
CHEDDAR PINK			
(Dianthus gratianopolitanus) **Nat(R)**	Early summer	20cm (8in)	Moths, butterflies
COMMON PINK			
(Dianthus plumarius) **Nat**	Summer	20cm (8in)	Bees
HAIRY THYME			
(Thymus praecox) **Nat**	Summer	8–10cm (3–4in)	Bees
HAREBELL			
(Campanula rotundifolia) **Nat**	Late summer	30cm (12in)	Bees
HEBE 'AUTUMN GLORY'			
	Autumn	60–90cm (2–3ft) (60–90cm/2–3ft spread)	Butterflies
HEBE 'CARL TESCHNER'			
	Summer	30cm (12in) (60–90cm/2–3ft spread)	Hoverflies, bees
HERB ROBERT			
(Geranium robertianum) **Nat**	Summer	30cm (12in)	Bees
LING (HEATHER)			
(Calluna vulgaris) **Nat**	Late summer	30–60cm (12–24in)	Ground cover for birds, grass snakes and slow worms
PURPLE SAXIFRAGE			
(Saxifraga oppositifolia) **Nat**	Summer	8cm (3in)	Butterflies, bees
ROCK ROSE			
(Helianthemum nummularium) **Nat**	Summer	15cm (6in) (60cm/24in spread)	Bees, insects
SPRING GENTIAN			
(Gentiana verna) **Nat(R)**	Spring	8cm (3in)	Butterflies, bees

Nat = native or naturalised
(R) = rare in the wild

MAKING A NEW WALL 'OLD'
New walls can be encouraged to take on an aged look and support more creatures. The main problem is that the mortar tends to be too hard to allow any insects to get into the crevices between the bricks. The answer is to drill a few carefully placed holes in the mortar to encourage mason bees and other insects to colonise. The surface of the brick can be 'weathered' by painting on a mixture of yoghurt (or milk and flour paste) and organic liquid manure, such as liquid seaweed. The surface will soon attract algae, mosses and other tiny plants.

continued on page 72

plants
OF THE
month

RAGGED ROBIN
(Lychnis flos-cuculi)

This pretty native plant of wet meadows and marshland makes a good garden plant for damp soils and wetlands. 'Ragged' probably refers to the petals which are cut into segments, giving a fringed, ragged appearance.

type	Perennial
flowers	Pink, early summer
height	60cm (2ft)
planting	Put out young plants in spring or autumn
site	Sun or partial shade, wetlands, pond margins, damp meadows
soil	Moist, fertile
care	Cut back flowering stems in mid-summer (after flowering) to encourage a second flush of flowers in late summer
propagation	Self-seeds readily. Plants may also be increased by division in spring
wildlife value	Long-tongued bees, flies and many species of butterflies (including whites and the common blue) seek out the pollen and nectar. Ragged robin is an essential ingredient of wetlands and marshy pool margins

COMMON EVENING PRIMROSE
(Oenothera biennis)

Originating from North America, the evening primrose has become naturalised on waste ground, railway embankments and road verges. It is not related to the primrose family *(Primula)* and was probably named because of the similarity in colour. Both the common and large-flowered species produce a mass of flowers. Each flower only lasts a day, opening in the evening to give off a light fragrance.

RAGGED ROBIN

type	Biennial
flowers	Yellow, summer/early autumn
height	1m (3ft)
planting	Plant out in autumn or spring, 30cm (12in) apart
site	Full sun, in borders
soil	Well drained
care	No special care needed
propagation	Self-seeds very easily. Seed may also be sown in late spring or early summer to flower the following year (seeds will sometimes germinate in spring and flower the same summer)
related species	The large-flowered evening primrose *O. glaxioviana* is a taller plant (1.5m/5ft), easily identifiable by its large flowers and red hairs on the stem. Widely cultivated in gardens and naturalised on disturbed ground
wildlife value	Evening primroses rely on moths for their pollination, hence the nocturnal opening hours of the flowers. The moths are attracted by the pale colour and also by the scent and are rewarded with nectar. Although the flowers only open at dusk, they usually last until noon the next day, allowing hoverflies time to visit the plant

FOXGLOVE
(Digitalis purpurea)

A tall-growing native of open woodlands and scrub. *D. purpurea* is very poisonous and the drug extracted from the plant is still used to treat heart conditions.

type	Biennial
flowers	Pink to purple, occasionally white, spotted interior, early to mid-summer
height	1.2m (4ft)
planting	Plant foxgloves between mid-autumn and early spring
site	Partial shade, in open woodlands, or shady borders
soil	Any, moist
care	No special care needed
propagation	From seed sown in early to mid-summer
wildlife value	The leaves provide food for butterfly caterpillars and the flowers are visited by pollen-seeking bumble bees

FOXGLOVE

practical
project

PLANTING WALLS AND
ROCK BANKS

FLOWERING WALL PLANTS

plant	season	height	flowers
SMALL-LEAVED COTONEASTER			
(*C. microphyllus*) **F**	Summer	6m (2½in) (2m/6ft spread)	White (scarlet berries)
HOARY CINQUEFOIL			
(*Potentilla argentea*) **N, B**	Summer to early autumn	30cm (12in)	Yellow
HOUSELEEK			
(*Sempervivum tectorum*) **I**	Summer	8cm (3in)	Red-purple
IVY-LEAVED TOADFLAX			
(*Cymbalaria muralis*) **N, B**	Summer	10cm (4in) trailing	Lilac with yellow markings
LONDON PRIDE			
(*Saxifraga* x *urbinum*) **N**	Summer	15cm (6in)	Pink
RED VALERIAN			
(*Centranthus ruber*) **Nat**	Summer	60cm (24in)	Red, pink or white
ROUND-LEAVED CRANESBILL			
(*Geranium rotundifolium*) **Nat**	Summer	15cm (6in)	Pink
STONECROPS			
Biting stonecrop (*Sedum acre*) **Nat, N**	Summer	10cm (4in)	Yellow
White stonecrop (*Sedum album*) **Nat, N**	Summer	10cm (4in)	White
WALLFLOWER			
(*Cheiranthus cheiri*) **N, Nat**	Spring to early summer	30cm (12in)	Yellow to orange-brown
WALL ROCKET			
(*Diplotaxis tenuifolia*) **B, Nat**	Late spring to early autumn	60cm (24in)	Yellow
ARABIS			
(*Arabis albida*) **B, N**	Late spring to mid summer	15cm (6in)	White
YELLOW CORYDALIS			
(*Corydalis lutea*)	Summer to early autumn	15cm (6in)	Yellow

PLANTING IN GRAVEL AND PAVING

Many plants enjoy the dry growing conditions and reflected warmth of gravel, stone chippings or paving. It is relatively easy to incorporate native species into existing paving schemes or to lay areas of gravel.

Making a gravel bed

- The underlying soil should be well-drained and gritty. If it is too heavy, mix it with equal parts of rock chippings or gravel.

- Cover the area with a layer of sand 2.5cm (1in) deep.

- Finish the bed with a 2.5cm (1in) layer of gravel or 0.5cm (¼in) stone chippings.

- Water plants well before removing them from their pots. Use a narrow trowel to make holes the same size as the root ball and firm them in gently.

- Water new plants thoroughly and sprinkle more gravel over the surface if necessary.

Planting in paving

If new paths or patios are to be laid, it is worth considering leaving some gaps

NOTE

- *Many plants will self-seed readily in gravel, and in a short time the gravel will have a natural, 'unplanted' appearance. Any weeds, such as groundsel, that also self-seed freely can be removed by hand* ∎

between the paving stones as planting pockets. If the stones are already laid, it is still possible to incorporate a wide range of species.

The simplest way is to take up some of the stones, perhaps to create a chequerboard effect. This is better done in a random pattern, rather than taking out every other stone. The earth beneath the stones should be workable and weed-free. Dig out the earth to a depth of 15–23cm (6–9in) and mix with an equal quantity of gravel or stone chippings. Replace the soil mixture and plant in the normal way.

Brick paths or patios can be planted in the same way. Take out any bricks that are already damaged or crumbling and fill the gaps as above.

PLANTS FOR PAVING AND GRAVEL

The following plants will thrive in a shallow, well-drained soil in full sun and will self-seed easily:

BROOM Nat, B
(Cytisus scoparius)

COMMON TOADFLAX Nat, B
(Linaria vulgaris)

GLOBE THISTLE B, N
(Echinops sphaerocephalus)

GREAT MULLEIN Nat, I
(Verbascum phlomoides)

HAWKWEED Nat
(Hieracium murorum)

LADY'S BEDSTRAW Nat
(Galium verum)

MAIDEN PINK Nat
(Dianthus deltoides)

THYME B
(Thymus spp.) **Especially the native Thymus praecox**

TRAILING ST JOHN'S WORT Nat
(Hypericum humifusum)

WHITE CAMPION Nat
(Siline latifolia)

YARROW Nat
(Achillea millefolium)

JULY

Food supplies are plentiful this month at every level of the garden ecosystem. As the flower borders reach their peak, nectar keeps bees and butterflies contented and new generations of caterpillars feed on the abundant leaves. At ground level the rising population of slugs and beetles is quickly devoured by young hedgehogs. Fox cubs, now above ground after several months in the earth are practising their hunting skills on garden voles and mice. So-called pests like aphids and midges are also at their peak but are scooped up in huge numbers by bats, blue tits and swallows.

But it is at night that the garden really comes to life. So many of the night-scented plants are in flower now, beckoning moths and butterflies with their sweet smell. Honeysuckle, evening primrose, night-scented stock and nicotiana attract not only with their scent, but also with their pale light-reflecting colours. Bat watching can also be rewarding, with possible sunset sightings of the larger noctules and, in the south of Britain, serotines.

Although there is plenty of food available, garden wildlife can suffer in hot dry spells from lack of water. Pond levels drop and marshy areas may dry out altogether. In the long term, the wetland habitat will not suffer as long as rain comes in the autumn, but extra dishes of water and bird baths are always welcome.

Native plants tend to be more resilient to dry spells than garden hybrids, although there are exceptions; imports from the Mediterranean like rosemary and thyme will positively thrive in a near-drought situation. A wildlife garden does not usually need constant attention and as long as water supplies can be maintained, gardeners may go off on holiday with an easy mind.

tasks
FOR THE
month

C H E C K L I S T

- Water hanging baskets and containers daily
- Plant autumn-flowering bulbs
- Prune broom
- Cut the summer-flowering meadow
- Tie in climbers
- Feed container plants
- Trim rock plants
- Undertake a butterfly count
- Prune rambler roses

WATERING

It is vital to keep bird baths and water bowls topped up during the summer months. Pay special attention to container-grown plants and hanging baskets, which will need watering daily to prevent plants from dehydrating.

PLANTING AUTUMN-FLOWERING BULBS

The meadow saffron *(Colchicum autumnale)* – sometimes called autumn crocus – and the true autumn-flowering crocus *(Crocus speciosus)* can be planted now. Both species look best grown in bold groups, in well-drained soil and in an open position or under a deciduous tree. Use a trowel or specially designed bulb planter and set the bulbs 10cm (4in) deep and 20cm (8in) apart for colchicums, 10cm (4in) deep and 10cm (4in) apart for crocuses. Cover completely with earth and firm in place.

PRUNE BROOM

Broom *(Cytisus scoparius)* should be pruned annually

after it has finished flowering. Careful pruning will prevent the shrub becoming bare-stemmed and leggy.

▪ Using sharp secateurs, cut back all or most of the stems which have just flowered. Make the cut just above the point where the stem joins the old wood and where new shoots are developing.

▪ Take care not to cut into the old wood, as it does

not respond well to pruning and may fail to produce any new growth. Mature plants do tend to become hard-wooded after several years and, if pruning has no effect, it is best to discard them.

CUTTING THE SUMMER-FLOWERING MEADOW

Established meadows
This is the traditional hay-making time of year and a good time to give the established summer-flowering lawn or meadow its annual cut. When the best of the summer flowers are over, cut down the grass to 10cm (4in), using a hand or motor-scythe (both should be handled by an experienced user for safety purposes). Leave the cuttings to dry in place for a day or so, as this allows insects time to crawl back

SOWING BIENNIALS
It is not too late to sow seeds of biennial plants for flowering next spring and summer. Wallflowers, foxgloves, forget-me-not and sweet rocket may be sown outdoors now and put into their flowering positions in the autumn (see p64–5 for details).

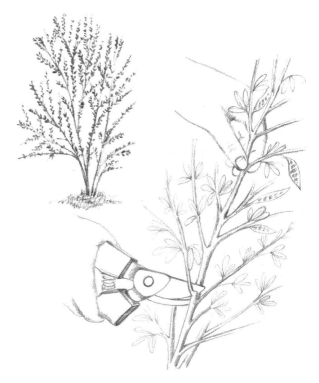

> **NOTE**
>
> ■ *Brooms are short-lived shrubs and should be discarded after six or seven years, when they become too woody and cease to flower* ■

into the meadow and any seeds to fall back to ground. Then, rake off the cuttings and add (sparingly) to the compost heap, or use as a mulch around trees and shrubs.

New meadows

Meadows sown last autumn with a mixture of meadow and annual cornfield flower seeds, should also be given their annual cut this month. If the cornfield annuals are still in flower, the cut can be left for a few weeks until they have finished. New lawns and meadows sown without the cornfield annuals should only be cut if particularly long and untidy (see p40 for more details on meadow maintenance).

TYING IN CLIMBERS

New growths of climbing plants such as honeysuckle or clematis should be trained towards their wires or trellis. If they are not tied in, the shoots become tangled and may not grow in the desired direction.

TRIMMING ROCK PLANTS

In small rock banks and walls, rock plants can soon outgrow their allotted space. As soon as they have finished flowering, cut back alyssum, aubretia, rock roses and pinks using secateurs for individual plants or shears for larger clumps. This will encourage new shoots to grow from the base.

PRUNING RAMBLER ROSES

The flexible stems of rambler roses make them excellent plants for growing over banks, through trees or in hedges, where they can be allowed to scramble unaided by trellis or ties. Unlike shrub and climbing roses, they bear their best flowers on the previous year's growth. Immediately after flowering (usually this month, although some varieties may not finish until late summer), cut out

> **NOTE**
>
> ■ *As the butterfly season gets into full swing, note down which plants are visited by which butterflies. Make a note to include more of these species next year* ■

the stems that have just borne flowers, leaving room for the young stems to come through. Use sharp secateurs and make clean cuts at ground level. Wear heavy duty gardening gloves to disentangle the prunings from the rest of the plant.

FEEDING CONTAINER PLANTS

This is the height of the growing season and plants in hanging baskets, tubs and window boxes should be given a liquid feed at fortnightly intervals. Alternatively, use pellets or tablets of slow-release fertiliser, which will provide enough nutrients to see the plants through to autumn.

THE BUTTERFLY COUNT

Use the garden's buddleias to carry out your own butterfly species count. It is remarkable how many will visit the flower spikes on a warm summer's day. Peacocks, tortoiseshells and red admirals are likely candidates, but painted ladies, wall browns and other less common species may well appear.

NATIVE BUTTERFLIES AND THEIR MAJOR SOURCES OF NECTAR

BRIMSTONE
Greater knapweed, thistles

COMMA
Michaelmas daisies, buddleia, sedum

COMMON BLUE
Field scabious, greater knapweed, red campion, ragged robin

HOLLY BLUE
Cotoneaster, ivy, holly

PEACOCK
Buddleia, Michaelmas daisies, sedum

RED ADMIRAL
Buddleia, Michaelmas daisies, sedum

SMALL TORTOISESHELL
Buddleia, Michaelmas daisies, sedum

SPECKLED WOOD
Bramble

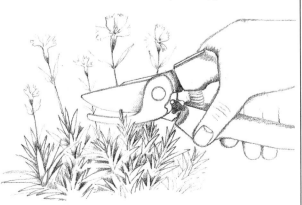

plants

OF THE

month

GREATER KNAPWEED
(Centaurea scabiosa)

A common wildflower, found on roadsides, hedgebanks and rough grass. The knapweed makes a good garden plant, with its bold thistle-like flowers which attract a good range of insects.

type	Perennial
flowers	Mauve/purple, mid- to late summer
height	60–90cm (2–3ft)
planting	Plant in early autumn or late winter
site	In full sun, as part of a flowering meadow or in a border
soil	Any, but prefers dry, chalky
care	No special care needed. Border plants can be lifted and divided every four years
propagation	Sow seeds as part of a meadow in early autumn. Established plants can be divided in late winter
related species	The common knapweed *(C. nigra)* is equally useful for wildlife although it is smaller and less impressive than *C. scabiosa*. Several of the non-native garden species are hardy and make useful tall border plants, such as *C. macrocephala* which has yellow flowers
wildlife value	The flowers are visited by bees, flying insects and particularly butterflies like brimstones. In early autumn the seedheads are eaten by finches

ROSE OF SHARON
(Hypericum calycinum)

Originating from Eastern Europe, *H. calycinum* is widely cultivated in gardens and naturalised in places in the countryside. As a garden plant it goes by the name of rose of Sharon but belongs to the same family as the wild St John's wort.

type	Evergreen sub-shrub
habit	Carpeting
flowers	Yellow, summer
height	30–45cm (12–18in)
spread	Indefinite
planting	Plant in early spring
site	Tolerates shade but flowers better with some sun. Borders, shrubberies or woodland edge
soil	Tolerates dry, poor soil. Can be grown in any well-drained garden soil
care	Every few years, cut plants back to within several centimetres or a few inches of the base to keep them compact
propagation	*H. calycinum* spreads by horizontal creeping stems and can soon outgrow its allotted space. To make new plants, lift and divide the roots in late winter
related species	The rock garden hypericum *(H. coris)* also appears this month and is useful for its yellow, heather-like flowers
wildlife value	*H. calycinum* is pollinated by bees who are attracted to the vivid yellow of the petals and the red-tipped anthers. It is a useful plant for a dry shady spot where it will effectively smother weeds

COMMON (OR FIELD) POPPY

COMMON (OR FIELD) POPPY

(Papaver rhoeas)

Formerly a frequent sight in cultivated fields, the common poppy is now increasingly confined to roadside verges and wasteland. It prefers ground which has been disturbed and occasionally makes an unexpected *en masse* appearance on motorway construction sites. In the garden it can be used to add temporary colour to a first year meadow or be sown with other annual 'cornfield weeds' on a piece of infertile ground.

type	Annual
flowers	Scarlet, summer
height	30–45cm (12–18in)
planting	Plant pot-grown specimens 30cm (12in) apart in mid- to late spring

	(Note: poppies are usually grown from seed, see 'Propagation' below)
site	Full sun. Disturbed ground such as a bonfire site or where an old shed used to be is ideal
soil	Prefers infertile, well-drained soil
care	No special care needed
propagation	Collect seed in late summer or early autumn and sow immediately as part of the flowering meadow. Alternatively store seed for sowing outdoors in mid-spring. Poppies self-seed very readily
wildlife value	Attractive to hoverflies and bees. Garden conservation is important as the increased use of weed-killers on agricultural land has led to their decline in the countryside

practical project

ESTABLISHING A 'NO GO' AREA

HEDGEHOGS
Don't feed hedgehogs in mid-summer. Left to their own devices, they will feed on garden slugs, helping to keep them under control.

However much we like to watch the comings and goings of the local wildlife, many creatures will only utilise the garden if there is one corner where they can remain totally undisturbed. It is important to nominate a part of the garden as a 'no-go' area for humans, which can be left deliberately untidy. Usually this is in some spot well away from the house and preferably shielded by shrubs or trees, but it might equally be behind a garden shed or garage.

THE WOODPILE

Old timber or unwanted logs can be piled up to provide shelter for a range of creatures. Choose a shady spot to prevent the wood from drying out in the sun. If possible, use a mixture of native woods such as elm, oak or ash which will guarantee a wider range of insect species. Logs 15–23cm (6–9in) in diameter make a good pile.

The first wildlife to inhabit the pile will probably be fungi in the early autumn, but in time it will become home to spiders, beetles, wood wasps, solitary bees, slugs and snails. These will then attract bird predators, particularly wrens and blackbirds, who will pick over the pile in search of a meal. The insects will also provide food for wood mice, voles and hedgehogs.

First-year newts, after leaving the pond, may well spend large amounts of time in the damp shelter of a log pile.

LEAF PILES AND HEDGEHOG HABITATS

If hedgehogs are to take up residence in the garden, they need a dry, secure place for hibernation from late autumn to early spring. A pile of dead leaves or garden prunings heaped into a corner will often be acceptable, but it is also possible to construct a hibernation 'box'.

■ Use an upturned wooden box (untreated wood) and cut an entrance out of one of the side panels, 10–12cm (4–5in) square. This is

PLAN AND SECTION OF HEDGEHOG HIBERNATION BOX

large enough to allow the hedgehog to enter but small enough to prevent dogs or foxes getting in.

■ A covered entrance tunnel can also be constructed using two rows of house bricks stood on their sides and a plank of wood. This helps to keep the interior of the box dry, but is not essential.

■ Cover the box with a sheet of polythene to keep out the rain, and a mound of dry leaves or brushwood to disguise the exterior. Add a handful of straw or dry leaves as bedding.

NETTLE PATCH

Stinging nettles are the caterpillar food plants for several native butterflies. Commas, peacocks, red admirals, and small tortoiseshells all rely on nettle leaves and shoots for their survival. If there is an existing nettle patch, this may need to be contained with a fence, wall or path. Better still, clumps of nettles can be transferred to large tubs or barrels sunk into the ground to prevent the roots from encroaching into the garden proper.

As the emerging caterpillars prefer fresh, new leaves to feed on, it is a good idea to cut back half the patch in early or mid-summer to encourage new growth. This is particularly important for commas and small tortoiseshells who regularly have two broods a year – the first in the spring, the second in mid-summer. The adults will seek out the new shoots to lay their eggs.

HABITAT BOOSTERS

A sheet of corrugated iron does not look very attractive, but if you happen to have one

WARNING

■ *Take care not to allow this 'wild' area to become used as a rubbish dump. Household rubbish such as open tin cans and broken bottles can be lethal to hedgehogs, foxes and other mammals who may try to eat or drink the contents, with serious consequences* ■

lying around, it is worth keeping. As the sun warms the metal, the 'tunnels' beneath become inviting resting quarters for slow worms and grass snakes. Equally, an old paving slab laid over a hollow in the ground and in a shady spot makes a damp hiding place for frogs and toads.

BRAMBLES – TO CULTIVATE OR NOT TO CULTIVATE

If ever conventional gardeners want to challenge their wildlife counterparts, the common bramble is more than likely to be held up as an example of irresponsible garden management. Bramble or wild blackberry *(Rubus fruticosus)* is present in many gardens, whether the owners want it or not and the question is, should gardeners be encouraging it, or should it be ripped out as an invasive nuisance?

As a wildlife plant, the bramble has enormous value. The flowers provide pollen for bees and nectar for butterflies all through the summer and it supports a wide range of smaller insects. The berries are a useful food supplement for small mammals and birds, as well as humans. It can be trained as a climber, to cover a wall or disguise unsightly outbuildings, and its dense, thorny growth makes excellent cover for nesting birds.

To set against this, it is an extremely difficult plant to control. A bramble thicket becomes almost impenetrable after a few years and the roots of established bushes are notoriously deeply anchored. Removing a bramble requires a combination of brute strength and endless patience as the tiniest piece of root left in the soil will spring back into life year after year.

It is not a good idea to introduce bramble into a small garden. There are plenty of equally good wildlife plants that do not swamp out other flora in the same way. However, if bramble already exists, one or two bushes could be retained, cutting out the old wood every other year and removing suckers and seedlings as soon as they appear. In larger gardens, a bramble patch can be accommodated, but will still need to be contained within its allotted space.

Bramble is a beautiful native plant of our hedgerows and woodlands, which fortunately is in no danger of extinction. While this is the case, perhaps we should be content to see it growing unrestrained in its natural habitat and fill the garden with less contentious plants.

NO GO AREA CHECKLIST

- ☐ **Log pile**
- ☐ **Nettle patch**
- ☐ **Leaf pile**
- ☐ **Hedgehog box**
- ☐ **Corrugated iron**
- ☐ **Old paving slabs**

GROWING NETTLES
Nettles can be introduced into the garden if they are not growing naturally. In late winter, dig up some roots about 4in (10cm) long which are bearing young shoots. Bury the roots in pots of garden soil and keep cutting back the shoots to 3in (7.5cm). By late spring the new plants can be put out into the untidy area.

plants
OF THE
month

NASTURTIUM
(Tropaeolum majus)

An import from South America, but nevertheless a quick-growing and useful garden plant. Trained to climb up a trellis or allowed to tumble over the sides of a window box, nasturtiums provide instant summer colour and considerable wildlife interest.

type	Annual
flowers	Orange/yellow, summer
height	2.5m (8ft)
habit	Climbing or trailing
planting	Plants should be set 40cm (16in) apart
training	Train plants up a 'wigwam' of canes or tie into a trellis. They can also be left to trail from a hanging basket or window box
site	Full sun, in containers, against fences and walls or in flower borders
soil	Prefers poor soil. A richer soil is tolerable but leaves may flourish at the expense of flowers
propagation	Sow seeds 2cm (¾in) deep in their flowering position in mid-spring. Thin out seedlings to 40cm (16in) apart
varieties	'Tom Thumb' is a dwarf variety (30cm/12in) suitable for edging paths or growing in a rock garden
wildlife value	Flowers attract bees and hoverflies. Leaves are eaten by the caterpillars of the cabbage white butterfly and other whites

NASTURTIUM

POT MARIGOLD
(Calendula officinalis)

A widely cultivated flower which often escapes onto wasteland where it thrives without any help at all. It is well worth including in the wildlife garden to increase the spectrum of yellow flowers sought after by flying insects.

type	Annual
flowers	Deep yellow/orange, summer to mid-autumn
height	60cm (24in)
planting	Grow from seed sown in flowering position in mid-spring. Cover seeds with 1cm (½in) soil. Thin out the seedlings to 30cm (12in) apart
site	Full sun, in borders or containers
soil	Tolerates poor, dry soil but flowers better in fertile garden soil or potting compost
care	No special care needed, but taking off the dead flowers will encourage plants to produce blooms for a longer period. Water containers in dry spells
propagation	If allowed to set seed, pot marigolds will produce numerous seedlings. These can be potted up or transplanted to other parts of the garden in spring. Otherwise sow seed outdoors in mid-spring
other species	The African and French marigolds *(Tagetes erecta* and *T. patula)* are also useful in the flower border for attracting butterflies. They are half-hardy annuals and can be bought as bedding plants in late spring
wildlife value	Pot marigolds can be grown in the vegetable patch as they are very successful in attracting hoverflies and wasps. Hoverfly larvae feed on aphids and wasps will devour caterpillars, providing a natural pest control system

RED CAMPION

FIELD SCABIOUS
(Knautia arvensis)

In the wild, field scabious is found growing on dry, chalky soils in meadows and hedgebanks. It makes a striking if somewhat leggy border plant and probably looks its best amongst grasses in a summer-flowering meadow.

type	Perennial
flowers	Mauve, mid-summer to early autumn
height	60–90cm (2–3ft)
planting	Plant pot-grown seedlings in autumn, directly into the meadow or border
site	Full sun, wildflower lawn, meadow or border
soil	Prefers light, well-drained soil, but will thrive in most garden soils
care	No special care needed
propagation	From seed sown outdoors in autumn or spring
related species	The small scabious *(Scabiosa columbaria)* (30cm/12in high) is a more compact relative of the field scabious. It can also be included in the meadow and looks less ungainly in the flower border
wildlife value	As part of a summer-flowering 'hay' meadow, both species of scabious attract several native butterflies, such as meadow browns, skippers, and common blues. Bees will also visit the plant for nectar

RED CAMPION
(Silene dioica)

A pretty native plant of open woodlands and hedgerows, the red campion adapts well to several garden situations. The flowers are actually pink rather than red, and in the wild it often hybridises with the white campion to produce an even paler colour.

type	Perennial
flowers	Rose-pink, late spring to early autumn (intermittently)
height	45–60cm (18–24in)
planting	Plant in autumn or spring, 15cm (6in) apart
site	Partial shade, in borders, beneath hedges or in woodland clearings
soil	Prefers a rich soil, but will thrive in ordinary garden soil
care	No special care needed
propagation	Sow seed outdoors in late spring. Young plants should be ready to go out in the garden in autumn. Red campion self-seeds profusely
related species	The flowers of the white campion *(S. latifolia)* open widest in the evenings, when they are most fragrant and attractive to moths and night-flying insects
wildlife value	Valuable nectar for butterflies

practical project

PLANNING A NECTAR-RICH FLOWER BORDER

Summer is a good time to plan a new border or to consider making an existing one more attractive to wildlife. Providing nectar is essential if you hope to attract butterflies. The sugary substance provides them with an important energy source during flight. Hopefully, as different species come in to feed on the flowers they will stay to breed and overwinter in the garden.

It is the scent and colour of flowers that signal to the butterflies that nectar is present. They seem to prefer heavy perfumes, but don't seem to be too fussy about colour.

Bees also feed on nectar (as well as collecting pollen to feed their young). Initially they are attracted by the scent and colour, but as they approach the flowers they are guided into the centre by markings on the petals – such as those on foxgloves and pansies – which are more apparent in the bees' ultra-violet vision.

There is no need to grow wild flowers exclusively in order to provide nectar. In fact, many of the garden-imported species and varieties are nectar-rich. Spend some time during the summer months studying your own garden and others you visit, making a note of which flowers are most attractive to bees and butterflies. From early autumn, many of the plants should be available as young pot-grown specimens in garden centres and nurseries.

Plant the border in autumn to give the plants a chance to get established before the cold weather comes. By spring, the border should be off to a good start.

NOTE

■ *The annual flowers: candytuft, tobacco plant and marigolds are placed near the front of the border where they can easily be taken out and replaced each year* ■

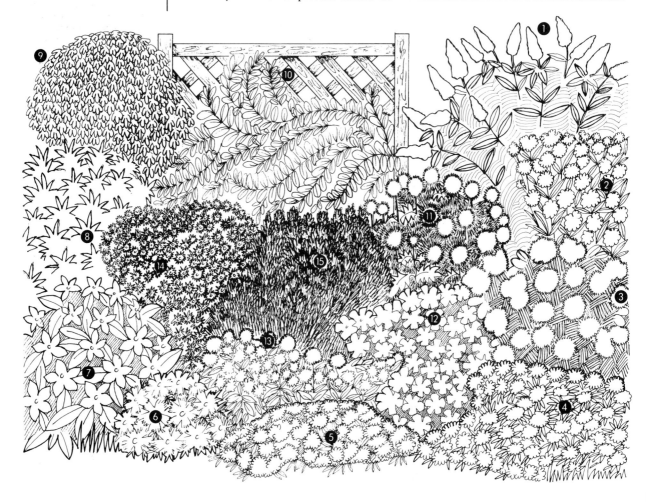

KEY: NECTAR-RICH FLOWER BORDER

plant	type/season	wildlife value
BUDDLEIA ❶		
(*Buddleia davidii*)	Shrub/late summer	Peacocks, whites, small tortoiseshells, commas, red admirals, brimstones
VERBENA ❷		
(*Verbena bonariensis*)	Perennial/summer to late autumn	Most butterfly species
SEDUM ❸		
(*Sedum spectabile*)	Perennial/autumn	Most butterfly species – especially small tortoiseshells, bumble-bees
CANDYTUFT ❹		
(*Iberis umbellata*)	Annual/summer	Most butterfly species
YELLOW ALYSSUM ❺		
(*Alyssum saxatile*)	Perennial/spring	Orange tips, small tortoiseshells, peacocks
FRENCH MARIGOLD ❻		
(*Tagetes patula*)	Annual/summer to autumn	Most butterfly species
TOBACCO PLANT ❼		
(*Nicotiana alata*)	Annual/summer	Moths – especially hawkmoths
GOLDEN ROD ❽		
(*Solidago canadensis*)	Perennial/autumn	Most butterfly species
FLOWERING CURRANT ❾		
(*Ribes sanguineum*)	Shrub/spring	Bees, early broods of butterflies
HONEYSUCKLE ❿		
(*Lonicera spp.*)	Climber/summer to autumn	Long-tongued moths, butterflies, bees
GLOBE THISTLE ⓫		
(*Echinops ritro*)	Perennial/summer	Bees
PHLOX ⓬		
(*Phlox paniculata*)	Perennial/summer	Most butterfly species, moths
RED VALERIAN ⓭		
(*Centranthus rubra*)	Perennial/summer to autumn	Hawkmoths, elephant hawkmoths, small tortoiseshells
MICHAELMAS DAISIES ⓮		
(*Aster novi-belgii*)	Perennial/autumn	Small coppers, tortoiseshells
LAVENDER ⓯		
(*Lavendula spp.*)	Shrub/summer to autumn	Meadow browns, late broods of whites, bees

FOOD FOR ALL
Each type of flower is designed to attract a different feeder. Those with flat, open flowers (such as roses) where the nectar is fully exposed are the province of flies and beetles. Bumble bees, with their fairly long tongues and hairy bodies, can prise open the flowers of snapdragons and bluebells. Those flowers which keep nectar at the base of a long tube (like red valerian) are only accessible to long-tongued butterflies and moths. However, all creatures are opportunists and will feed on whatever plants are available.

AUGUST

The pleasures of wildlife watching this month are heightened by the good weather. The garden is literally seething with activity as the warmer temperatures bring in greater numbers of hoverflies and ladybirds, both good friends to the wildlife gardener. Hot, humid conditions can trigger an invasion of both insects, who will earn their keep by keeping the greenfly population in check. One hoverfly may look much like another, but in fact around a hundred different species have been recorded in British gardens.

The surface of the pond will also be alive with new generations of darter dragonflies, water boatmen, and pond skaters. Tiny midge-like insects provide food, not only for the dragonflies but also for swifts and swallows who will scoop them up in thousands every day. Bats also make use of these feeding grounds, leaving their roosts at night to hunt for insects. With their young well matured, the females can leave the nursery sites again. Pipistrelles are the most common bats in urban areas, but near canals and rivers the Daubenton's bat is just as likely to be seen racing along the course of the water. In dry spells, the pond and surrounding marsh will be the focus of activity for mammals like hedgehogs and foxes who, exhausted by the heat, may forget their natural timidity and drink at the water's edge in broad daylight. Some birds can be seen drinking and washing in the pond, but overall this is an unrewarding time of the year for garden bird watching. Although the new broods of young will be boldly exploring their surroundings, the adults are more likely to be lying low in the undergrowth, undergoing their summer moult. Losing feathers makes flight difficult and most species tend to remain quietly hidden, hence the noticeable absence of birdsong.

tasks
FOR THE
month

CHECKLIST

- [ ] Take semi-hardwood cuttings
- [ ] Water containers and berry-bearing shrubs
- [ ] Set up pond alternatives
- [ ] Trim deciduous hedges

LAST-MINUTE PLANTING

This is the last chance to plant meadow saffron *(Colchicum autumnale)* and autumn crocus *(Crocus speciosus)* (see p76 for planting instructions)

TAKING SEMI-HARDWOOD CUTTINGS

Mid- to late summer is the time to take semi-hardwood cuttings of shrubs like lavender and ceanothus which do not root well from the more usual autumn hardwood cuttings. A semi-hardwood cutting is taken from the current year's growth which has begun to get woody towards the base but is still green and soft at the tip. They take a little more care than the hardwood cuttings, but the trouble is worthwhile for any shrubs that prove difficult to propagate.

TAKE EXTRA CUTTINGS
As not all cuttings will be successful it is worth taking a few extra cuttings from each shrub.

■ Choose this year's growth (easily identifiable as the shoots with leaves growing on them) and select a side shoot about 15–20cm (6–8in) long. Using secateurs, cut the shoot near to the point where it meets the main stem.

■ Using a sharp knife take off the lower leaves and trim the cutting just below a leaf joint. Take off the soft tip, just above a leaf joint so that the finished cutting is 5–10cm (2–4in) long.

■ Insert the cutting to one-third of its length in a small pot of seed or cuttings compost.

■ Water well with a fine sprayer and cover the pot with a polythene bag, secured with a rubber band. A plastic drinks bottle cut in half and placed over the pot also works well.

■ Place the pot in a warm place (16–18°C/61–64°F) but out of direct sunlight. The cuttings should root in two to three weeks.

■ Harden off the cuttings by gradually lifting the polythene to allow more air to circulate over the next three to four weeks.

■ Transfer the cuttings individually into larger pots. Place the pots in a cool greenhouse or coldframe and keep well watered. Plant outside in the spring.

WATERING

In any hot, dry spells container plants will need to be watered every day to stop them drying out. Pay special attention to hanging baskets and small pots. It is also worth watering berry-bearing shrubs like cotoneaster and pyracantha as lack of moisture can lead to a poor crop in the autumn. Frequent watering will help to swell the developing fruit.

POND ALTERNATIVES

Birds, too, can suffer in particularly dry summers. Check the pond level and top up if necessary. Rainwater is preferable if available from a barrel or waterbutt, as tapwater can lead to the growth of algae in the pond. If the garden does not have a pond, then it is vital to provide alternative wildlife drinking and washing places. An upturned dustbin lid balanced on two piles of bricks is one solution, or a washing-up bowl set into the soil so it is level with the ground. Even a large terracotta saucer or dish will suffice. Check the levels daily and fill up as necessary.

TRIMMING DECIDUOUS HEDGES

Native deciduous hedges (single species or mixed) can be clipped now. Overgrown hawthorn, beech, field maple or hornbeam will benefit from a trim, once the danger of disturbing nesting birds is past. Use sharp hedging shears and keep the blades flat against the face of the hedge. Cut the top of the hedge with the shears held horizontally. Electric hedgetrimmers are noisy and can cause accidents. Unless the length of hedge is great, hand shears give a less severe cut.

NOTE

■ *Native hedges do not need clipping every year and should only be clipped to retain shape and control over-exuberant growth* ■

TAKE SEMI-HARDWOOD CUTTINGS FROM THE FOLLOWING SHRUBS:

Barberry *(Berberis thunbergii)* F
Ceanothus
***(Ceanothus x burkwoodii)* N**
Firethorn *(Pyracantha)* F
Guelder rose *(Viburnum opulus)* F
Honeysuckle
***(Lonicera periclymenum)* N**
Japanese quince
***(Chaenomeles speciosa)* F**
Lavender *(Lavandula)* B, N
Rosemary
***(Rosmarinus officinalis)* B, N**
Shrubby cinquefoil
***(Potentilla fruticosa)* B, N**

plants
OF THE
month

WILD ANGELICA
(Angelica sylvestris)

Most at home in damp meadows, fens and on river banks, wild angelica is a widely distributed wild herb. The tall stems are distinguished from the more commonly grown garden angelica by their slender growth and purplish-pink colour. Wild angelica has a rather bitter taste but it makes a good architectural plant for the pond edge or marsh.

type	Perennial herb
flowers	White or pink, summer to autumn
height	2m (6ft)
planting	Plant in early spring, leaving 1m (3ft) between plants
site	Sun or partial shade, in marshy ground, by ponds or in damp meadows
soil	Damp, rich soil
care	Wild angelica is fairly shortlived, so plants can be discarded and replaced after two to three years
propagation	Self-seeds easily; or collect seed in early autumn, store and sow outdoors in spring
species and varieties	Garden angelica (*Angelica archangelica*) is now widely naturalised and is used to flavour liqueurs. The leaves are dried and used in teas and pot pourri
wildlife value	Both angelicas have wide, open flowerheads which makes them accessible to small insects like hoverflies. The seedheads also provide useful food for birds in late summer and early autumn

PURPLE LOOSESTRIFE
(Lythium salicaria)

A native flower of pond edges, marshes and wetlands. The spires of purple flowers are excellent for the wildlife garden, blooming throughout the summer.

type	Perennial
flowers	Purple, summer
height	1m (3ft)
planting	Plant young specimens in spring or autumn 45cm (18in) apart
site	Sun or partial shade at pond edge or wetland
soil	Moist
care	Divide roots in autumn if plant has outgrown its space
propagation	Self-seeds easily. May also be grown from purchased seed
wildlife value	Supplies nectar and pollen for bees and butterflies; caterpillars of the small hawkmoth feed on the leaves

LADY'S BEDSTRAW
(Galium verum)

A common wayside flower, found in grasslands, on sand dunes and road verges. Originally known as 'Our Lady's Bedstraw', it was reputed to have been used to scent the stable bedding in Bethlehem. The sweet-smelling dried flowerheads were traditionally added to the straw used to fill mattresses.

type	Perennial
flowers	Golden yellow, summer
height	45cm (18in)
habit	Sprawling
planting	Young pot-grown plants should be put out in autumn
site	Full sun, in a meadow or border
soil	Dry, poor
care	If grown as part of a meadow, the grass should be left uncut until early autumn
propagation	Lady's bedstraw will spread rapidly through a meadow without any intervention. It can also be grown from seed collected in early autumn or bought from a nursery
wildlife value	A valuable native constituent of the summer-flowering meadow. The strong scent attracts a wide variety of insects, particularly butterflies and hawkmoths

WILD ANGELICA

TREE MALLOW

TREE MALLOW
(Lavatera thuringiaca 'Rosea')

A vigorous shrub, often distrusted by gardeners because of its tendency to grow coarse and woody. It grows quickly, even on poor soils, to produce a large, handsome plant bearing masses of pink flowers that last right through the summer and well into autumn.

type	Semi-evergreen woody perennial
flowers	Rose-pink, mid-summer to late autumn
height	1.2m (4ft)
spread	1.2m (4ft)
planting	Put out young plants in spring or autumn, 1.2m (4ft) apart
site	Sun
soil	Any, well-drained
care	If plant starts to outgrow its space, cut stems back to ground level in early spring
propagation	From semi-hardwood cuttings in late summer
wildlife value	Bees, butterflies and flying insects flock to the open flowers which appear continuously for over four months of the year

SEA HOLLY
(Eryngium maritimum)

A hardy native perennial found growing on sands, rocks and shingle around the coasts of Britain. The distinctive spiky blue-green leaves and powder-blue flowers make the sea holly a popular border plant.

type	Perennial
flowers	Blue, mid-summer to early autumn
height	45cm (18in)
spread	30cm (12in)
planting	Young pot-grown plants should be planted 30cm (12in) apart between autumn and spring
site	Sun
soil	Well-drained
care	Cut stems to ground level in early spring
propagation	Sow seeds in spring
wildlife value	Bees, beetles and sometimes butterflies seek out the flowerheads for nectar

Herbs have been part of cultivated gardens for over two thousand years. Many of our most familiar herbs were introduced into the country at some point in history, but have been with us so long that to say they are not native is rather academic. Certainly many garden escapees have become naturalised and have adopted the countryside as their own. However purist we may be about using native plants, few gardeners would banish herbs from the garden. Not only have they a proven use in cooking and health treatments, but they are extremely decorative and blend in well with a natural-looking garden.

practical project

PLANNING A HERB BED OR GARDEN

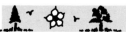

TOP HERBS FOR WILDLIFE

herb	type	wildlife value
ANGELICA		
(Angelica archangelica)	Biennial	Flowers – hoverflies, bees Leaves – butterflies, caterpillars Seedheads – greenfinches, bluetits
BORAGE		
(Borago officinalis) **Nat**	Annual	Flowers – bees
CHIVES		
(Allium schoenoprasum) **Nat**	Perennial	Flowers – bees, butterflies
COMFREY		
(Symphytum uplandicum) **Nat**	Perennial	Leaves – moths, butterflies
FENNEL		
(Foeniculum vulgare) **Nat**	Perennial	Flowers – bees, wasps, hoverflies Leaves – caterpillars
HYSSOP		
(Hyssopus officinalis) **Nat**	Perennial	Flowers – lacewings, bees
LAVENDER		
(Lavandula angustifolia)	Shrub	Flowers – bees, butterflies
MARJORAM		
(Origanum vulgare) **Nat**	Perennial	Flowers – bees, butterflies
MINT		
(Mentha – all types) **Nat**	Perennial	Flowers – bees, butterflies, moths
ROSEMARY		
(Rosmarinus officinalis)	Shrub	Flowers – bees, butterflies, hoverflies
THYME		
(Thymus – all types) **Nat**	Perennial/small shrub	Flowers – bees, butterflies

LEAVE HERBS TO FLOWER
Herbs that are grown primarily for their leaves, either for cooking or medicine, usually have their flowerheads removed to encourage consistent leaf growth. Instead of snipping off the flowers as they appear, leave a few plants of parsley, mint, marjoram and lemon balm to flower naturally. Many more insects will visit the plants and consequently the herb garden will be a richer feeding ground for birds.

TOP HERBS FOR WILDLIFE

Although there are a huge number of culinary and medicinal herbs which can be grown, not all are relevant to wildlife. The chart on p92 describes the best herbs for attracting garden wildlife.

PREPARING THE SITE

The best location for a herb bed is one which gets a lot of sun and where the soil is already well drained. Most herbs dislike getting waterlogged roots and can tolerate almost drought conditions – in fact, those like rosemary and marjoram with Mediterranean ancestry, improve in taste, scent and flower growth in a sunny location.

■ If the soil is not ideal (heavy clay for instance), it is possible to add some coarse grit to aid drainage. However, it might be simpler and more productive to grow the herbs in pots, putting in a good layer of gravel before adding the compost.

■ The ground should be dug thoroughly, removing any weeds and large stones. Lay brick paths, edging tiles or wooden dividers before planting the herbs.

HERBS FOR LESS-THAN-IDEAL CONDITIONS

Although most herbs prefer a sunny position in a well-drained soil, there are some which will tolerate shade and a heavier soil. The resulting plants may not do as well but there is no need to give up the idea of growing herbs altogether and the wildlife will still find them useful.

■ Mint *(Mentha)* can tolerate shade although it does tend to grow towards the light and become crooked and leggy.

■ Tansy *(Tanacetum vulgare)* is an excellent native plant for butterflies and it is not too fussy about growing conditions.

■ Lovage *(Levisticum officinale)*, a relative of the fennel, is also worth growing for its young leaves which add a celery flavour to soups and stews. It will grow quite adequately in a dark, damp spot and the flowers produced,

PLANTING AND MAINTENANCE CALENDAR

LATE SUMMER

Prepare site

AUTUMN

Plant shrubs and pot-grown perennials

SPRING

Sow seeds of annuals

LATE SPRING

Sow seeds of biennials

SUMMER

Keep beds free of weeds; water container plants

although not as abundant as they should be, will provide nectar for hoverflies, wasps and bees.

■ Comfrey *(Symphytum × uplandicum)* should be included purely for its leaves which are a reliable food source for moth and butterfly caterpillars.

■ Lemon balm *(Melissa officinalis)* is another strong grower in less than ideal conditions. Its white or pale yellow flowers rely on bees for their pollination.

■ Garden chervil *(Anthriscus cerefolium)* is an annual herb, greatly prized for the flavour of its parsley-like leaves. It will tolerate some shade, but prefers a well-drained soil.

■ Great burnet *(Sanguisorba officinalis)* is a tall native herb that prefers a damp habitat and a heavy clay soil. The tiny crimson flowers appear from mid-summer through to early autumn.

■ Angelica *(Angelica archangelica)*, originally from central Europe, is widely naturalised in Britain. It will do well in a shady spot in damp soil and has huge seedheads in early autumn. *(Continued on page 96.)*

plants
OF THE
month

BELLFLOWERS
The bellflowers, or campanulas,
belong to a huge family of plants,
almost all with the characteristic
bell-shaped flowers. They range
from the giant bellflower
(C. lactiflora) reaching 1.5m (5ft)
in height, to the tiny fairy's thimble
(C. cochlearifolia) which grows
in the rock crevices of its native
Alps. All bellflowers, including our
native harebell, are pollinated by
bees.

HAREBELL
(Campanula rotundifolia)

Known in Scotland as the bluebell, it is in fact a completely different species to the English bluebell *(Scilla non-scripta)*. The harebell is a widespread native of sand dunes, grassy banks, heaths and downs and is often cultivated in gardens for its pretty bell-shaped flowers.

type	Perennial
flowers	Blue, occasionally white, mid- to late summer
height	30cm (12in)
planting	Plant out pot-grown specimens in early autumn or spring
site	Sun or partial shade. In flowering meadows, borders, dry-stone walls, rock gardens and containers
soil	Poor, dry soil preferred but will tolerate normal border soil
care	If grown in a meadow, wait until early autumn before cutting
propagation	From seed collected in early autumn
related species	Most of the garden campanula species, although not native, are useful for attracting insects. *C. lactiflora* makes an attractive, tall border plant and *C. carpatica* can be grown on walls and in rock gardens where it forms a compact mat
wildlife value	Harebells rely on bees for pollination and are attractive to most flying insects. As part of a summer-flowering meadow they will attract many different species of butterfly including small whites

HEATHER
(Calluna vulgaris)

The heather family *(Ericaceae)* includes a large group of heaths and heathers, which are found growing wild on the moorlands, woods and bogs of Britain. They make excellent plants for a wildlife garden, provided the soil is not too limy. The summer-flowering heather or ling *(C. vulgaris)* gives good ground cover to birds, insects and reptiles.

type	Sub-shrub
flowers	Lilac to pale purple, mid- to late summer
height	30–60cm (12–24in)
spread	30–60cm (12–24in)
planting	Plant in groups, during spring or in late autumn. Space the plants 45cm (18in) apart. Make sure the roots are buried deeply and the foliage rests on the soil surface. Water after planting and during any dry spells for the first year of growth
site	Open, sunny site in borders, rock gardens or containers
soil	Prefers a peat-based, acid soil. If the garden soil tends towards lime, it is best not to try to grow heathers, and not add peat artificially
care	Mulching around the roots will prevent water loss. The flowerheads can be left on the plants through the winter and clipped off in the spring to encourage new growth
propagation	By semi-hardwood cuttings taken in late summer
varieties	There are many garden hybrids available, all of which will provide good cover for wildlife. *C. vulgaris* 'Golden Haze' is a white-flowered variety with particularly attractive golden foliage
wildlife value	The spreading, low-growing mounds offer protection to ground-feeding birds like wrens and the insects they are seeking. Grass snakes and slow-worms may seek out the sun-soaked patches between the plants, where they are safe from human feet

GLOBE THISTLE
(Echinops ritro)

Originating from southern Europe, the globe thistle has long been cultivated in British gardens. The thistle-like leaves are in fact downy underneath and not at all prickly. The globe-shaped, steel blue flowerheads make this an attractive border plant with the added bonus that bees seem to love it.

type	Perennial
flowers	Blue, late summer, early autumn
height	1–1.2m (3–4ft)
planting	Set out young plants in autumn or spring, 60cm (24in) apart
site	Sunny, in borders
soil	Well-drained
care	Cut back stems to ground level in spring to make room for new growth. (Leave the seedheads intact through autumn and winter)
propagation	Lift and divide plants in autumn or spring
wildlife value	Bumble bees and many species of butterfly seem to enjoy extracting the nectar from the short tubular flowers. The seedheads are popular with finches in autumn and winter

GLOBE THISTLE

practical project

PLANNING A HERB BED OR GARDEN

MINT
The four different varieties of mint are contained in narrow segments to prevent them over-running the entire bed

PLANNING THE HERB GARDEN

For human requirements, it is useful to have all the herbs grouped together within easy reach of the kitchen or back door. Wildlife, on the other hand, will happily seek out their favourite herbs wherever they are planted. If it is not practical to make a special herb bed, individual plants can be incorporated into the general garden planting. Thyme, for example, grows well over an old stone wall and rosemary could be included in a sunny shrub border. If space is limited, one solution might be to plant the herbs in pots, window boxes or troughs. However, if there is room, it is very satisfying to devote a special part of the garden to herb growing. This can be any shape at all: linear rows (like a vegetable plot) perhaps divided by a lavender hedge; a circle divided into segments to keep the different species apart; a rectangular plot intersected by paths to allow easy maintenance; or a more ambitious knot garden, marked out with clipped box edging.

A HERB WHEEL

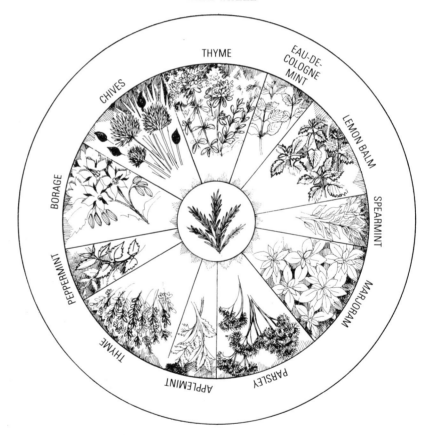

RECTANGULAR PLOT INTERSECTED BY PATHS

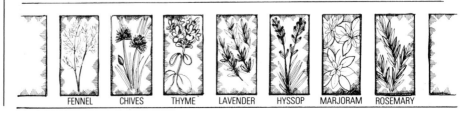

FENNEL · CHIVES · THYME · LAVENDER · HYSSOP · MARJORAM · ROSEMARY

TRADITIONAL HERB GARDEN LAYOUTS

SEEDS FOR THE BIRDS
Chicory, angelica, lovage and fennel all provide an accessible supply of bird seed after they have finished flowering

Paths may be paving, grass, bricks or gravel

BUTTERFLY NECTAR
Hyssop, lavender, catmint, marjoram and thyme flowers are useful sources of nectar for summer butterflies

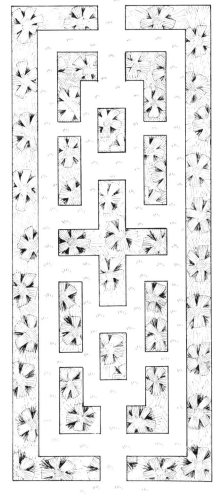

STONE BIRDBATH

LOW-GROWING HERBS
Choose low-growing herbs: thyme, chives, dwarf lavender and marjoram

Underplanted with herb segments divided by stones

SEPTEMBER

This part of the year, when summer draws to a close and moves ever closer to autumn, is one of the most enjoyable times in the wildlife garden calendar. All of the bird species should be more in evidence after their late summer moult, and birdsong fills the air once more. The days are still warm, and long enough for the gardener to stay outside until dusk, when bats can often be seen circling overhead, catching insects in flight.

There should still be dragonflies dancing over any marshy areas or ponds and this is a good time for butterfly watching, as the third generation of adults emerge to take advantage of the late summer flowers. In woodland areas, the speckled wood butterfly may also be seen fluttering in the dappled sunlight.

In the bird kingdom, this is the start of the outward migration period, clearing the airways for the influx of continental visitors due next month. Swifts and swallows announce their departure south with aerial displays of divebombing, accompanied by loud screeching. Their close cousins, the house martins, seem more reluctant to leave and often hang on for another month or two.

Other species starting to depart now include the garden and willow warblers, blackcaps and pied flycatchers.

Native hedgerows are bursting with hips and berries, making rewarding hunting grounds for moths, insects, birds and small mammals. The wild blackberry, or bramble, is also at its peak, bearing luscious edible fruits, but it is planted at the gardener's peril. It is a matter of weighing up the hours of backbreaking work needed to dig out the bushes when they inevitably begin to take over, against the undoubted wildlife benefits of the fruit, flowers and thorny stems which give such good protection to nesting birds.

tasks

FOR THE

month

BUTTERFLY BUSHES
Snip off the faded flowers of
buddleia bushes now to
encourage them to keep on
flowering. Many butterfly species
will visit the bush well into the
autumn.

CHECKLIST

- Last cut for the meadow/wildflower lawn
- Harvest fruit
- Plant evergreen shrubs and trees
- Clear annual flower beds
- Collect seed

FINAL MOWING OF THE WILDFLOWER LAWN

Lawns or meadows that have been left uncut to allow later flowering species to develop can be mown now. Use a rotary mower, heavy duty strimmer or a hand scythe and cut the grass to leave 8cm (3in) of stubble. Leave the cuttings on the ground for a day or two to allow insects to find their way back to ground, then rake them off and add to the compost heap.

WARNING

■ *Strimmers and scythes can be extremely dangerous if handled incorrectly. If in doubt, get help from someone who is experienced in the use of agricultural tools* ■

THE FRUIT HARVEST

Traditional gardeners are gathering in the harvest of fruits and vegetables now, eating some and storing the rest away for use later in the winter. Try leaving some plums and pears on the tree where, as they soften and become more juicy, they will attract butterflies galore. Instead

of taking all the apple crop indoors for storage, leave at least half the fruit intact to provide on-tree and windfallen fare for hungry birds. Some of the stored crop can be kept until

---

mid-winter, when it can be strewn on the lawn to attract visiting redwings.

USING EVERGREEN SHRUBS AND TREES

The ubiquitous conifer has been so overused in conventional gardens that wildlife gardeners tend to treat all evergreens with disdain. Yet, a carefully chosen selection of evergreen trees and shrubs can provide some unexpected benefits for wildlife, not to mention an

USEFUL EVERGREENS

name	wildlife value
COTONEASTER	
(C. dammeri, C. simonsii C. microphyllus)	*Abundant berries*
FIRETHORN	
(Pyracantha – species and hybrids)	*Winter berries and spring flowers*
HOLLY	
(Ilex aquifolium) **Nat**	*Secure nesting and berries*
OREGON GRAPE	
(Mahonia aquifolium)	*Early flowers for nectar and autumn berries*
SCOTS PINE	
(Pinus sylvestris) **Nat**	*Crossbills prise the seed from pine cones*
VIBURNUM	
(Viburnum tinus)	*Early flowers for nectar*
YEW	
(Taxus baccata) **Nat**	*Makes an excellent nesting hedge*

important structural component of the garden.

The yew, Scots pine and holly are all native evergreens well worth including if space allows, while ornamental shrubs like viburnums, mahonias and the evergreen cotoneasters carry useful flowers and berries which add to the food stock available to wildlife.

PLANTING EVERGREEN SHRUBS

■ Dig a hole as deep as, and slightly wider than, the shrub's container. Loosen the soil at the bottom of the hole with a fork and add a handful of garden compost.

■ Place the shrub in the hole, checking that the soil will cover it to the same depth as it did in the container (bare-root plants should have a soil mark on the stem).

■ Fill the hole with loose soil, tread down firmly and add more soil if necessary. Tread the soil down again.

■ Water the soil around the shrub thoroughly so that it soaks right down to the roots.

NOTE

■ If grown as a tree rather than a hedge, yew can reach 20m (65ft) and Scots pine frequently 40m (130ft), so these species should only be considered for large gardens. They can be planted this month and planting instructions are as for deciduous trees (see Planting a Woodland Habitat/Practical Project/October*) ■*

CLEARING ANNUAL FLOWER BEDS

Many annual flowers are coming to the end of their life and the space may be needed for other plants. The most common procedure at this stage is to clear the flower beds completely and deposit the dying plants on the compost heap. However, there are some annuals, like sunflowers, that produce seed which the birds love. If the bed must be cleared, a good compromise is to cut off the seedheads first, tie them in a bunch and hang them from a windowsill, fence or from a low branch away from cats, where they will still be accessible to greenfinches and other seed eaters.

COLLECTING SEED

Annual seed can also be collected now for sowing next year. Snip off entire seedheads and place them upside down in a paper bag. If the seeds are ripe, a few shakes of the bag should dislodge them. Spread the contents of the bag onto a tray and separate out the seeds. Pour into airtight containers (glass herb jars work well), and don't forget to label them before storing in a cool, dark place until spring.

Seed may also be collected from perennials to increase your stock of wildlife plants for borders, meadow and wetland. Ragged robin, greater knapweed, lady's bedstraw and field scabious can all be propagated from seed.

FLOWERS FOR SEED COLLECTION

Corncockle (Agrostemma githago)
Evening primrose (Oenothera biennis)
Larkspur (Delphinium consolida)
Night-scented stock (Matthiola bicornis)
Poppy (Papaver rhoeas)
Teasel (Dipsacus fullonum)
Sunflower (Helianthus annuus)

TESTING FOR RIPENESS
Seeds are 'ripe' when they come away freely from the flowerhead, after the flower has faded. If the seeds do not shake free easily, put the heads into a paper bag and hang in a dry place for up to two weeks, until the seeds fall naturally to the bottom of the bag.

plants
OF THE
month

ELDER
(Sambucus nigra)

The native elder grows prodigiously on waste and scrublands, in woods and on riverbanks. People and wildlife compete for its favours, as both flowers and fruit are used in winemaking and the fruit is particularly rich in vitamin C.

type	Deciduous shrub or small tree
flowers	Creamy white, mid-summer
fruits	Black berries, early autumn
height	To 4m (13ft)
spread	3.6m (12ft)
planting	Plant young trees between mid-autumn and early spring
position	Sun or partial shade. As part of a mixed hedge, shrubbery or woodland edge
soil	Fertile
care	No pruning necessary. Elder can be coppiced in winter but no flowers or berries will be produced the following year
propagation	Take hardwood cuttings in mid-autumn for planting out a year later
varieties	The golden elder, *S. nigra* 'Aurea', is worth growing for the golden colour of the young leaves
wildlife value	Mainly grown for its rich crop of berries which are amongst the first shrub or hedgerow fruits to ripen. Most of the resident garden birds will feast on the berry-laden branches. The summer flowers are also a useful nectar source for insects

GOLDEN ROD
(Solidago canadensis)

This species was introduced from North America and is now widely naturalised, as well as being a popular garden plant. It is one of the essential components of a traditional herbaceous border. The smaller, native golden rod (*S. virgaurea*) flowers earlier and is not as well known, although seed can be obtained from some wildflower nurseries.

type	Perennial
flowers	Yellow plumes, late summer to mid-autumn
height	1–1.5m (3–5ft)
spread	1m (3ft)
planting	Plant between mid-autumn and early spring, 0.6m (2ft) apart
position	Sun or partial shade, in borders
soil	Any
care	No special care needed. Tall plants may need staking
propagation	Divide plants in autumn or late winter, or grow from seeds sown in spring. Golden rod also self-seeds very readily
varieties	Hundreds of varieties are available derived from *S. canadensis* and *S. virgaurea*. 'Golden Thumb' is a good dwarf variety, 30cm (12in) high. Other full-size varieties worth growing are 'Golden Gates' and 'Cloth of Gold'
wildlife value	Very attractive to moths, as well as a wide range of other insect species. The fluffy seedheads later in the autumn are particularly relished by seed-eating birds

ELDER

SEDUM
(Sedum spectabile)

Sedum spectabile is an exotic member of the stonecrop family which, as the name suggests, inhabits rocky locations in many areas. The garden sedums, however, can be grown in any ordinary soil and are some of the best wildlife plants for the flower border.

type	Perennial
flowers	Pink, crimson or mauve, autumn
height	30–45cm (12–18in)
planting	Plant between autumn and early spring, 45cm (18in) apart
position	Full sun in borders, rock gardens or containers
soil	Well-drained
care	Sedums are resistant to drought so should not need extra watering
propagation	Divide and replant between mid-autumn and early spring
varieties	'Autumn Joy' is a delicate, salmon-pink in colour; 'Brilliant' is a stronger shade
wildlife value	Small tortoiseshell butterflies flock to sedum, as do most insects in search of nectar. The wide flowerheads remain intact into late autumn, when most flowers in the border have run to seed

TEASEL
(Dipsacus fullonum)

The wild teasel makes a good garden border plant, establishing itself in many different kinds of habitat and providing a wide range of wildlife interest. The closely related Fuller's teasel (*D. fullonum* subsp. *sativus*) is still cultivated commercially for its hard spiky seedheads which are used to raise the nap of fine worsted cloth in traditional weaving mills.

type	Biennial
flowers	Pink/purple, mid-summer
seed	Brown, spiny seedheads, early autumn
height	To 2m (6ft 6in)
planting	Plant out small pot-grown plants in mid-autumn
position	Open, sunny position in flower borders
soil	Any
care	No special care needed
propagation	By seed collected in autumn and sown in spring. As teasel is biennial, the spikes will not appear until the second year. It self-seeds quite readily

wildlife value   The huge, honeycombed seedheads will be flocked by goldfinches each autumn, teasing out the seed with their beaks. Earlier in the year the bracts around the stem form a reservoir, which attracts insects and small birds to drink the collected rainwater. Although the flowers are short-lived, they attract bees and a good range of butterflies, including the common blue and small copper

TEASEL

practical project

CREATING A SUMMER-FLOWERING MEADOW

This is the best time of year to think about making a wildflower meadow to flower next summer. By sowing seeds now, they will have the best chance of becoming established through the autumn and winter. Wildflower seeds can either be sown on bare ground, or incorporated into an existing lawn.

SOWING A WILDFLOWER LAWN

Choosing the site

Many wildlife gardeners prefer to keep some of the grassy areas of their garden as conventional lawn and it makes sense to mow the grass closest to the house. A wildflower meadow could be created in any other part of the garden, perhaps beyond the short grass or bordering a woodland area. Choose an area that has not been heavily fertilised – a vegetable patch would not be suitable, but a neglected lawn which has received no feeding or chemicals would be. It is best to avoid sites with a history of persistent weeds like docks and thistles. Choose a sunny location, away from too many overhanging trees.

Ground preparation

This is probably the most important part of the whole operation. Meadow flowers and grasses will only establish themselves on ground with low fertility, so this needs to be given some consideration. One way of reducing soil fertility is to remove the top layer of turf, and possibly the topsoil as well. Dig over thoroughly or cover the area for a complete season with black polythene to ensure all perennial weeds are eradicated.

Choosing a seed mixture

For most situations, a standard meadow mixture containing 20% flower seed and 80% grass seed will be adequate. A typical summer-flowering meadow mixture might include musk mallow, bird's foot trefoil, knapweed and lady's bedstraw, along with a selection of bent and fescue grasses. Good seed merchants will list the exact proportions of all the constituents of their mixtures. There is also a range of mixtures designed specifically for unusual growing conditions such as particularly sandy or chalky soils or damp, marshy ground.

The meadow mixture can either be sown alone or mixed with some annual cornfield flower seeds. This is termed 'nursing' and, although it is not strictly necessary, the annuals will provide cover for the developing perennials, which take longer to establish. This method has the added advantage of giving a bright display of poppies and cornflowers in the first year.

PLAN FOR THE SITE OF A WILDFLOWER MEADOW

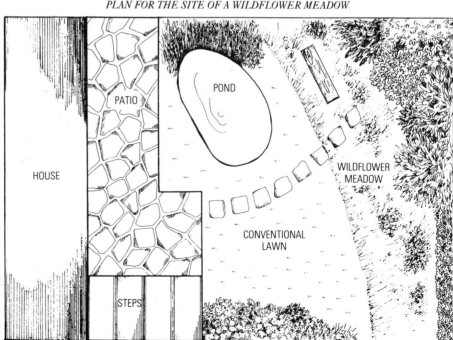

HOUSE

PATIO

POND

WILDFLOWER MEADOW

CONVENTIONAL LAWN

STEPS

SOWING THE SEED

■ Remove all large stones from the earth and rake it thoroughly. Sieve the soil through a large garden sieve if necessary, to produce a fine tilth. Continue raking and treading the surface until it is absolutely level.

■ Water the ground with a sprinkler hose or a watering-can with a fine rose until soaked.

■ Mix together the meadow and annual seeds (if used). Sow the seed thinly – a rough guide is 4gm per square metre (⅛oz per 10sq ft), but check the instructions for each particular mixture. To ensure an even coverage, walk the plot in one direction, sowing at only half the recommended rate. Then walk the plot in the opposite direction, sowing the remainder of the seed. The seed can be broadcast by hand and it will be easier to spread if mixed with a little silver sand before sowing.

AFTERCARE IN THE FIRST YEAR

Meadow mixture only
Make the first cut when the grass is over 10cm (4in) high (usually about six weeks from the start of the spring growing season). Then cut monthly or as often as necessary to keep the site tidy. On poor soils there may not be much growth and only occasional cutting will be necessary. Remove the cuttings to prevent an increase in fertility.

Meadow mixture sown with cornfield annuals
Cut the grass once only, in late summer, after the annuals have flowered. Remove the cuttings after mowing.

MEADOW MAINTENANCE IN LATER YEARS

The traditional rhythm of meadow maintenance, still practised by a few farmers, is quite straightforward: an annual cut of the meadows in late summer for hay, followed by grazing of livestock through the autumn and winter. This sort of seasonal pattern works just as well for a wildflower lawn, cutting the grass grass once after the summer display. As far as winter grazing is concerned, mowing occasionally through the autumn and winter will achieve a similar effect.

However, it is quite simple to vary the peak flowering period by changing the mowing regime – an earlier cut will encourage more spring-flowering species like cowslips and fritillaries, whilst a later cut benefits the late-flowering knapweeds and field scabious.

INCORPORATING WILDFLOWERS INTO AN EXISTING LAWN

There are basically two ways of doing this, both of which can be implemented in early autumn. The first involves sowing seed, the second planting pot-grown plants. Whichever method is chosen, the best results will be obtained with a lawn that is already patchy and weak in growth. The lush green grass of a well-fed lawn is likely to swamp any wildflowers that are introduced.

Sowing wildflower seed into an existing lawn
Begin by giving the lawn a thorough raking with a metal rake to remove moss, dead grass and leaves. Water thoroughly and sow the seeds at the manufacturer's recommended rate.

Adding pot-grown wildflowers to an existing lawn
After the last cut of the season is a good time to put in pot-grown wildflowers. More and more nurseries are stocking wildflowers in pots, but remember to choose species which will suit your intended regime of meadow maintenance. Place the plants in groups, with individual plants 20-40cm (8-16in) apart. Remove a plug of earth the same size as the pot, using a bulb planter or trowel. Knock the plants from their pots and place them in the holes, firming down the soil and watering well afterwards.

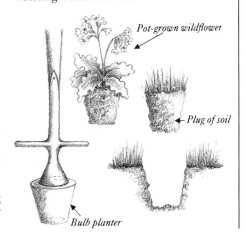

Pot-grown wildflower

Plug of soil

Bulb planter

TYPICAL MEADOW MIXTURE

20% Flowering native perennials *(as below)*
40% Crested dog-tail *(native grass)*
30% Fescue *(non-native grass)*
10% Bent *(lawn grass)*

SPRING-FLOWERING MEADOW PERENNIALS

Bladder campion *(Silene vulgaris)*
Cowslip *(Primula veris)*
Lady's bedstraw *(Galium verum)*
Meadow buttercup *(Ranunculus acris)*

SUMMER-FLOWERING MEADOW PERENNIALS

Betony *(Stachys officinalis)*
Bird's foot trefoil *(Lotus corniculatus)*
Field scabious *(Knautia arvensis)*
Greater knapweed *(Centaurea scabiosa)*
Meadow cranesbill *(Geranium pratense)*
Musk mallow *(Malva moschata)*
Ox-eye daisy *(Leucanthemum vulgare)*
Rough hawkbit *(Leontodon hispidus)*
Selfheal *(Prunella vulgaris)*

O C T O B E R

This is the season of misty mornings and warm afternoons when
the garden enjoys the last rays of the summer sun. For conventional
gardeners it is one of the most productive times of the whole year,
preparing for the major planting period ahead. In the wildlife
garden, this is also an important planning and planting time, not
only to establish the structure of next year's garden, but to ensure
that the resident creatures have everything necessary to keep them
going through the winter.

If the weather holds, the flower borders will go on supplying nectar
for insects and seedheads for birds for some time yet. Hebe
'Autumn Glory', sedums, Michaelmas daisies and any late
racemes of buddleia will be thronging with butterflies taking a last
draught before overwintering amongst the plants and shrubs.
Mature specimens of climbing ivy are bearing flowers now, and
will host many species of butterfly. In particular the holly blue is
worth looking out for. As the name suggests, these butterflies lay
their spring eggs on holly bushes, but the autumn brood of
caterpillars feed exclusively on the shoots and flowers of ivy, where
they will also remain as chrysalises throughout the winter.

In most parts of the country it is not cold enough to put out bird
food and there are plenty of seasonal berries, nuts and seeds
available. Unlike hibernating mammals, birds do not generally
store up food to see them through the winter. One exception to this
is the jay, which can be seen carrying away acorns to bury under
the soil. The acorns eventually germinate and the green shoots
appearing above ground enable the jay to relocate the acorn later
in the winter.

tasks

FOR THE

month

next month (see p120).

CHECKLIST

- Plant spring-flowering bulbs
- Plant out biennials and perennials
- Mulch beds and borders
- Take hardwood cuttings
- Sow tree and shrub seeds

BULB PLANTING 1

The majority of spring-flowering bulbs can be planted now, although one or two are better left until next month (see p120). Bulbs are one of the easiest ways to ensure a good supply of late winter and spring flowers, providing early nectar for insects, bees and butterflies.

The bulbs chosen may be a mixture of native and exotic varieties and, according to type, may be planted in lawns and grassy banks, in flower beds and containers, or under hedgerows and trees. Bulbs look best growing in natural drifts and this effect can be achieved by throwing a handful of bulbs onto the ground and planting them where they fall. If planting in grass, use a specially designed bulb planter (in earth, a trowel works better) to remove a plug of soil. The

LEAVE WINDFALL APPLES
Don't collect all the windfallen apples for eating or storing. Leave them on the ground instead where the soft fruit will attract ground-feeding birds like blackbirds, as well as providing a late source of energy for butterflies before they overwinter amongst the garden foliage.

RECOMMENDED BULBS

name	site	planting depth
BLUEBELL		
(*Scilla non-scripta*) **Nat, B, N**	*Hedgerows, woodland*	*5cm (2in)*
CROCUS (PURPLE)		
(*Crocus tomasinianus*) **N**	*Lawns, borders, under deciduous trees*	*8cm (3in)*
CROCUS (YELLOW)		
(*Crocus chrysanthus*) **N**	*Lawns, borders, under deciduous trees*	*8cm (3in)*
GRAPE HYACINTH		
(*Muscari neglectum*) **Nat, B, N**	*Lawns, borders*	*8cm (3in)*
RAMSONS GARLIC		
(*Allium ursinum*) **Nat, N**	*Hedgerows, woodland*	*8cm (3in)*
SNOWDROP		
(*Galanthus nivalis*) **Nat**	*Under deciduous trees, shady borders*	*5cm (2in)*
WILD DAFFODIL		
(*Narcissus pseudonarcissus*) **Nat, B**	*Lawns, banks*	*8cm (3in)*
WINTER ACONITE		
(*Eranthis hyemalis*) **Nat**	*Under deciduous trees, shady borders*	*5cm (2in)*

Planting depth = depth of soil *above* the bulb

hole should be approximately twice as deep as the bulb itself. Insert the bulb in the hole, point upwards. Replace the plug of earth and firm in.

Newly planted bulbs, particularly wild varieties, may take two to three years to get established and flower freely.

PLANTING OUT BIENNIALS AND PERENNIALS

This is a good month to put in some of next year's border flowers, particularly any that have been grown from seed in the spring.

Biennial wallflowers, sweet william and foxgloves are tried and trusted cottage-garden flowers that will make a big contribution to the reservoir of nectar, pollen and seed in the coming spring and summer. Container-grown border perennials such as globe thistle, sedum, Michaelmas daisies and hellebores are also good for wildlife and may be planted now.

These plants can be left until spring if you prefer, but an autumn planting will give the roots a good chance of establishing

NOTE

- *Bear in mind that these plants may be only a fraction of their full-grown size. Check the size of each species and allow enough room for plants to grow – plants put in too close together will compete for air, sunlight and nutrients and may develop poorly as a result* ■

before the cold weather comes.

Follow the steps below for the best results.

Planting steps

- Choose the site according to each plant's soil and light requirements.

- Ensure the soil is in a workable condition – turn over with a fork or add garden compost to improve fertility if necessary.

- Tap the plants out of their pots. Make a hole with a trowel or spade, slightly bigger than the root ball.

- Place the plant in the hole, making sure the bottom of the stem is level with the soil in the bed.

- Fill around the roots with loose soil and firm in.

AUTUMN MULCHING

Permanent shrub or herbaceous borders will benefit from a mulch (a shallow top layer) of garden compost or well-rotted manure. A layer of organic matter can also be spread over empty beds, where it will improve the soil and keep the area weed free until it is replanted. The autumn rains help to take nutrients down into the soil and the extra material will boost the wildlife habitat at ground level, increasing the insect population and making the borders a good feeding ground for birds.

TAKING HARDWOOD CUTTINGS

The simplest way of propagating most deciduous shrubs and trees is by hardwood cuttings, taken when the plants are just starting their period of winter dormancy.

Take several cuttings at the same time, from different shrubs, and prepare a nursery bed where they can grow on undisturbed for twelve months. Choose a sheltered site, and dig over thoroughly, removing any weeds and stones.

continued on page 112

PLANTS FROM WHICH TO TAKE HARDWOOD CUTTINGS

Broom
(Cytisus scoparius)
Flowering currant
(Ribes sanguineum)
Honeysuckle
(Lonicera periclymenum)
Elder
(Sambucus nigra)
Ivy
(Hedera helix)
Wild privet
(Ligustrum ovalifolium)
Willow
(Salix spp.)

plants
OF THE
month

IVY

(Hedera helix)

IVY – ALL YEAR ROUND
AUTUMN
nectar for hoverflies and butterflies

WINTER
shelter for overwintering butterflies and berries for birds

SPRING
nesting site for wrens and blackbirds, young leaves for caterpillars

SUMMER
cool roosts and nesting sites

The common ivy is a hardy climber and one of the real stalwarts of the garden. It is a native plant and can also be found growing widely in woodlands, hedgerows or clambering up the walls of disused buildings. It is a better choice for the wildlife garden than the Canary Island ivy *(H. canariensis)* which is often sold in garden centres. Although a good strong climber, *H. canariensis* does not attract the same range of insects.

type	Evergreen climber
flowers	Yellow-green, autumn
fruits	Green berries, turning black when ripe in mid-winter
height	Up to 30m (100ft)
habit	Self-clinging, climbing or trailing
planting	Put in young plants between early autumn and early spring. (Container-grown plants may be planted at any time of the year.) Water well during first few months, particularly if grown against a wall or in poor soil

site	Partial shade or shade, against fences and walls, on trellises or up old trees, as ground cover or in pots. Prefers some shade, especially from the mid-summer sun, but will tolerate most situations
soil	Any
care	No special care needed. Ivies grown against the house may need to be cut back to avoid gutters and windows – do this in early winter, after flowering and before nesting birds move in
propagation	From cuttings taken in autumn
varieties	There are hundreds of named varieties and as far as wildlife is concerned it does not really matter which are grown although native ones are preferable
wildlife value	Flowers produce a supply of nectar throughout the autumn and will be visited by hoverflies, holly blue and tortoiseshell butterflies. As winter comes, the leaves give shelter to overwintering butterflies and in spring the new shoots provide food for emerging caterpillars. Because the berries ripen later than other fruit-bearing bushes, they will be eaten eagerly by resident birds and winter visitors. Once established, wall-trained ivies provide nesting sites for wrens, house sparrows and blackbirds

ROWAN OR MOUNTAIN ASH
(Sorbus aucuparia)

The mountain ash or rowan is a widespread native tree of woodlands, moors and mountains. With its frothy clusters of flowers and distinctive berries it is one of the basic requirements for the woodland area of a wildlife garden. In the Scottish Highlands, it used to be planted by houses to ward off witchcraft and it is still a popular tree for municipal planting.

type	Deciduous tree
flowers	Creamy white, late spring, early summer
fruits	Orange-red berries, autumn. Rich in vitamin C, they make a good jelly
height	10–15m (30–50ft)
planting	Plant young trees between mid-autumn and early spring
site	In sun or partial shade. Suitable for a narrow woodland belt or planting individually. It is also tolerant of exposed positions
soil	Prefers a well-drained, acid soil
care	No pruning or special care. Can be coppiced
propagation	Usually seedlings spring up wherever birds deposit the seeds. Can also be grown from seed taken from the berries in autumn
varieties	The dwarf rowan *(S. aucuparia* 'Fastigiata') is a useful variety for the smaller garden. It has the same berries and flowers but grows to only 4m (13ft)
wildlife value	As the berries start to ripen they are devoured by the resident bird population, particularly blackbirds, well before the winter visitors arrive. The early summer flowers are nectar-rich and rely on insects for their pollination. There are over twenty insect species specifically associated with the rowan tree. Beware of planting the similar-looking Japanese or American rowans, which will not support the same range of insects

WHITEBEAM
A close relative of the rowan and another good tree for the wildlife garden is the common whitebeam (Sorbus aria). It can reach a height of 25m (80ft) in full maturity, so it is only really suitable for the largest gardens. However, if there is space, this tree does grow on a chalky soil, which the rowan does not, and is equally attractive to birds and insects.

ROWAN BERRIES

tasks
FOR THE
month

PROPAGATING TREES AND
SHRUBS
Seeds or cuttings?
Taking hard and softwood
cuttings is certainly the easiest
and most reliable way to increase
your stock, but the resulting plants
will be identical to the parents. In
the wild, trees and shrubs spring
up naturally from seed and
contain a great deal of interesting
genetic variation. It is worth
having a go at collecting seed, just
to see what turns up.

Taking the Cuttings
Look for vigorous stems that have just completed a season of growth. They will be hard and woody, with healthy buds all along the length of the stem.

■ Using sharp secateurs, cut the stem from the plant near the point where it joins the main branch or stem.

■ Using a sharp knife, trim the cutting to 25–30cm (10–12in), cutting just below a bud or leaf joint at the bottom, and just above a bud or leaf joint at the top.

■ To encourage rooting, cut away a thin piece of bark from one side of the base.

Planting the cuttings
■ Make a trench in the prepared ground by pushing in a spade and pulling it forwards several inches, to form a narrow, v-shaped trench.

■ Put a 3–5cm (1¼–2in) layer of coarse sand at the

bottom to ensure good drainage. Place the cuttings on the sand so that half to two-thirds of the cutting will be below ground level. Set the cuttings 8–10cm (3–4in) apart. Fill the trench with soil and firm down.

Aftercare
The cuttings should not be disturbed for a full twelve months. If cuttings are 'lifted' by the frost, push them down again gently, so that the base is once again in contact with the sand at the bottom of the trench. Watering will only be needed in particularly dry spells – most likely in the summer months. Keep the area weed free.

By the following autumn, the cuttings should have rooted and have a few sets of leaves. These can be lifted and transplanted to their permanent positions in the garden. If space is limited, they may be put into adequate-sized pots and grown on for one or two years. Any cuttings that have not rooted should be left in position for another year.

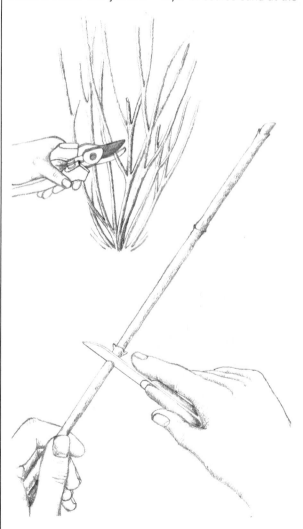

GROWING TREES AND SHRUBS FROM SEED

Autumn is the best time to collect tree seeds and berries for propagation. Growing from seed can sometimes be a slow and erratic process, but it is very rewarding in terms of the variety of seedlings produced. Rowan, alder, hazel, elder, shrub roses, hawthorn, guelder rose, blackthorn and most native trees can be grown in this way.

Collecting the seed

Seed should be collected as soon as it is ripe and sown immediately. Seeds which are contained within fleshy fruits, such as rosehips and elderberries, should be squeezed out of their soft casing before sowing. (The seeds of many of these berry-bearing shrubs and trees will only germinate in the wild when they have been eaten, digested and deposited by birds or mammals.)

Stratification

Many seeds have a hard outer coating which will prevent germination unless it is broken down by any one of the methods known generally as stratification.

NOTE

- *Some trees take several years to germinate successfully (particularly if there is not a sufficiently cold 'snap' in winter). Keep the pots outdoors for two to three seasons before discarding them* ■

The simplest way of doing this is to expose the seeds to a period of intense cold which will break down the protective layer. Any seeds which prove difficult to germinate should be sown and the pots left outside for the winter, in a position which is exposed to the action of ice and frost.

Alternatively, the outer coating of large seeds can be damaged by making a little cut in each seed with a sharp penknife. For smaller seeds, rub them between two sheets of sandpaper.

Sowing the seed

Individual seeds should be put into 15cm (6in) pots of proprietary seed compost or a sandy soil, so they lie 2.5cm (1in) beneath the surface of the compost. Stand the pots in a coldframe or cool greenhouse until the following spring. (Most species will germinate in this way, but any that prove difficult should be exposed to frost, as above.)

As soon as the seeds show signs of growth in the spring, move the pots out into a partially shaded place in the garden. (The seedlings need plenty of light, but should not be exposed to direct sunlight, particularly in the summer months.) Keep the compost moist and grow on, transplanting to bigger pots as necessary. Young trees should be planted out into their permanent positions in autumn, two years after sowing.

COLLECTING SEEDS FROM NUTS, HIPS AND BERRIES

Alder *(Alnus glutinosa)*
Hard, green clusters. Collect before they turn brown and woody

Blackthorn *(Prunus spinosa)*
Blue-black, downy fruit. Squeeze flesh to remove seed

Elder *(Sambucus nigra)*
Black berries. Squeeze to remove seed

Guelder Rose *(Viburnum opulus)*
Bright red berries. Squeeze to remove seed

Hawthorn *(Crataegus monogyna)*
Dull red berries. Each berry contains only one seed

Hazel *(Corylus avellana)*
Hard cobnuts. They are ripe for collecting when they change from green to brown

Rowan *(Sorbus aucuparia)*
Red berries. Squeeze fruit to remove seed

Shrub roses *(Rosa spp.)*
Red hips. Mash to a pulp and leave to dry before extracting seed

plants
OF THE
month

MICHAELMAS DAISY
(*Aster novae-angliae* and *Aster novi-belgii*)

The Michaelmas daisy is not a native flower, having been imported from North America around 1710, but it is now naturalised in many parts of Britain. The original species went out of favour in the Victorian era, because the flowers were not thought to hold their own amongst some of the bolder occupants of the flower border. Their revival must in some part be due to William Robinson who in his un-orthodox book *The Wild Garden*, written in 1870, lovingly depicted the Michaelmas daisies growing naturally in the woodlands and clearings of New England, and urged readers to find a place for them in the domestic garden.

type	Perennial
flowers	Violet petals with a yellow central disc. Hundreds of named varieties in shades of pink, blue, red and purple. Early to mid-autumn
height	Varies according to variety 45cm–1.2m (18in–4ft)
planting	Plant young plants 40cm (15in) apart, between mid-autumn and early spring
site	Open, sunny site, in a flower border or clearing between trees
soil	Fertile, well drained
care	Make sure plants do not dry out during flowering. Divide and replant clumps every two or three years as they take a lot of nourishment from the ground and tend to deteriorate if not moved. Remember to discard any diseased or weak plants. Taller varieties

TRUE QUINCE
The true quince tree, Cydonia oblonga, *is a relative of the ornamental* Chaenomeles. *Grown for its apple- or pear-shaped fruits, it makes an attractive garden tree. Gather some of the fruit in early autumn, before the first frosts, and leave the remainder for birds and late butterflies.*

JAPANESE QUINCE
(*Chaenomeles speciosa*)

Originating from China and Japan, *C. speciosa* has a role to play in the wildlife garden. In a small space it can be trained against a fence, where it will start blossoming in late winter in mild districts and bear fruit throughout the autumn. Like the true quince, the fruits can be used for preserves.

type	Deciduous shrub
flowers	Red, pink, white, early to mid-spring
fruits	Fragrant, yellow-green, edible fruits, autumn
height	1.8m (6ft)
spread	1.8m (6ft)
planting	Plant bare-root specimens between mid-autumn and early spring. Container-grown plants can be put in at any time except mid-summer
site	Full sun, trained against a wall or fence
soil	Any
care	Prune after flowering, in mid- to late spring
propagation	By semi-hardwood cuttings in late summer
varieties	Many garden varieties available. Choose single rather than double forms. 'Apple Blossom' is a popular variety with white flowers tinged with pink
wildlife value	Spring flowers are attractive to bees and butterflies. Fruit-fall in autumn is eaten by ground-feeding birds (thrushes and blackbirds)

propagation | may need supporting with bamboo canes or twigs
Divide and replant pieces of healthy root taken from the outside of the clump in mid-autumn or late winter

varieties | Michaelmas daisies tend to be prone to mildew, although the species seem more resistant than some of the highly bred varieties. The insects and butterflies however seem not to mind which are planted

wildlife value | Provides some of the last nectar of the season, which is particularly important for overwintering butterflies like the tortoiseshells, commas and brimstones

MEADOW SAFFRON
(Colchicum autumnale)

This native flowering bulb is commonly found in grassy meadows and on the edge of woodlands. It is sometimes called the autumn crocus and often confused with the autumn-flowering members of the true crocus family, which look rather similar, although the colchicum's leaves are broader.

type | Bulb
flowers | Pink, lilac, autumn
height | Flowers: 15cm (6in); leaves: 25cm (10in)
planting | Plant bulbs in late summer/early autumn, 10cm (4in) deep and 20cm (8in) apart. Plant in groups of five or more
site | Sun or partial shade. In rough grass, woodland edge, borders or containers
soil | Well drained
care | No special care needed. Can be left in position for many years
propagation | Divide the clumps in mid-summer, separating and replanting the offsets
varieties | A white form, *C. autumnale* 'Album' is also available
wildlife value | Bumble bees and butterflies visit the brightly coloured flowers to collect nectar and build up food reserves before the onset of winter

AUTUMN CROCUS
(Crocus speciosus)
The true autumn crocus, although not native, is also worth growing for its bright lilac-blue flowers, heavy with nectar. Planting and cultivation instructions are the same as for the colchicum, although as the crocus has less prominent leaves, the bulbs can be planted closer together, 8–10cm (3–4in). Many garden varieties are available, including a white form, C. speciosus 'Albus'.

MEADOW SAFFRON

practical project

PLANNING AND PLANTING A WOODLAND HABITAT

*THE CLASSIC WOODLAND
STRUCTURE*
*An ideal woodland would consist
of one or two dominant trees such
as beech or oak, underplanted
with a canopy of smaller trees like
field maple, crab apple and birch.
Beneath this would be a shrub
layer, composed of hazel, guelder
rose and holly. On the woodland
floor primroses, bluebells, violets
and wild garlic would flourish
along with the mosses, lichens
and fungi which are essential to
the ecology of the woodland.*

Even the smallest garden can incorporate a woodland habitat. Most of the natural deciduous woods in Britain have been traditionally managed, by coppicing for example. The resulting woodlands are not dark, dense forests, but a series of open glades, copses or woodland-edge habitats, where light is allowed to reach the woodland floor and a wider range of flora and fauna can exist. Beetles, wood wasps, slugs and spiders will make up the insect population, which in turn will attract hedgehogs, wood mice, ground-feeding wrens and blackbirds. The native trees should attract a wider number of birds species than before, including jays hunting acorns in autumn and perhaps nightingales in summer.

SITING THE WOODLAND

It makes sense to utilise what trees are already in the garden and build the woodland around these. The end of the garden is a logical place for a woodland, or along the boundaries. An existing shrubbery would be another starting point – unwanted shrubs could be removed and replaced with species which will attract more wildlife. The orientation of the woodland does not matter too much, although it is best to avoid a south-facing position which might get too much sun.

CHOOSING THE TREES AND SHRUBS

Think in terms of a three-tier system. The top layer is the larger 'forest' trees. The second layer is made up of small trees and the third layer is the woodland shrubs. In a small garden only layers two and three are planted – the small trees become the top canopy and the shrubs become the underplanting. Choosing native trees and shrubs is always preferable, simply because they support a greater range of insects and associated wildlife. However, any garden species which are useful to wildlife can be included.

WHAT TO LOOK FOR WHEN BUYING TREES

Choose young trees, 1–2m (3–6ft) in height, and look for a strong central upward-growing shoot and a healthy root system. Beware of trees which have had their central growing

tip pinched out. This is often done to encourage side shooting, to make the sapling look more like a little tree, but it inhibits natural upward growth. Young trees are best bought from a specialist tree nursery. If possible, choose the specimens yourself rather than have them sent by mail.

PLANTING THE WOODLAND

Having chosen the piece of ground where the woodland is to be created, the first task is to clear the area of any rubbish or debris. Lift any unwanted plants and shrubs into pots, ready for replanting elsewhere. There is no need to dig over the ground unless, for example, it is full of builders' rubble.

As a general rule, trees and shrubs should be planted 2–3m (6–10ft) apart. Before digging any holes, it is a good idea to have a trial run, placing the saplings in position on top of the earth and moving them around as necessary until you are happy with the layout.

Tree planting

■ Dig a hole about 1m (3ft) across and deep enough to ensure the sapling will sit at the same depth as it did in the nursery. (For container-grown specimens this is the depth of the pot; for bare-root trees, look for a soil mark on the stem.) Loosen the soil in the hole with a fork and add a spadeful of garden compost if available.

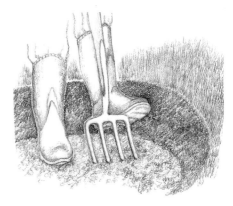

■ Use a stout wooden stake which should reach just below where the tree starts to branch. Drive the stake into the centre of the planting hole, as deeply as possible, and hammer in place with a mallet.

- Part-fill the hole with loose soil and position the tree in the hole, placing a piece of wood across the top of the hole. The old soil mark should be level with the piece of wood.

- Continue filling in the hole, shaking the tree occasionally to make sure the soil settles between the roots.

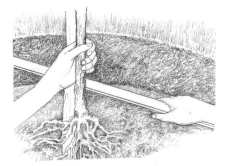

- Tread the soil down firmly, adding more soil if necessary to give a level finish.

- Use a rubber tree-tie to fix the tree to the stake about 10cm (4in) below any side branches. Choose a tie which has a small rubber

buffer attached – this prevents the vulnerable stem from rubbing against the stake.

For shrub planting, follow instructions on p101 'Planting Evergreen Shrubs'.

Aftercare

Newly planted trees should be checked regularly during the winter to make sure they have not become dislodged by wind or frost, and that the ties are still in place. As the tree stems thicken, the ties should be loosened to accommodate this growth. In hot or dry weather, trees in their first few years of growth should be watered regularly. It is also important to keep competing seedlings and weeds at bay, to give new trees and shrubs the best chance of survival.

THE WOODLAND FLOOR

You can speed up the process of woodland creation by importing some of the ingredients of a natural woodland floor. Leaf mould will build up gradually as the trees and shrubs grow and shed their leaves, but for the first year, a layer of leaf mould spread around the saplings will enrich the soil. Likewise a layer of coarse bark looks natural, makes a good mulch and keeps weeds at bay.

WOODLAND FLOWERS

It is best to let the trees and shrubs establish themselves for a year or two before planting woodland flowers. At first the gaps will be too large between the trees and there will not be the shade necessary to grow most species. Once the canopy layers have developed, however, there are many woodland plants which can be introduced in the autumn.

WOODLAND MAINTENANCE

During the first five years of a woodland's life, the trees and shrubs will jostle for space and light. By watching the way different species grow, you will soon spot those that need to be halted in their growth or taken out altogether. Coppicing (see p129) is a good way of keeping shrubs in check or, if that seems too drastic, selective pruning of specimens that have outgrown their allotted space will suffice.

RECOMMENDED WOODLAND PLANTS

LAYER 1: LARGE TREES
Beech *(Fagus sylvatica)* I, F
Elm *(Ulmus procera)* I
Oak *(Quercus robur)* I, F
Lime *(Tilia cordata)* I
Hornbeam *(Carpinus betulus)* I
White willow *(Salix alba)* I
Wild cherry *(Prunus avium)* F, N

LAYER 2: SMALL/MEDIUM TREES
Alder *(Alnus glutinosa)* S
Silver birch *(Betula pendula)* I
Downy birch *(Betula pubescens)* I
Field maple *(Acer campestre)* I

LAYER 3: SHRUBS
Bird cherry *(Prunus padus)* F, N
Crab apple *(Malus sylvestris)* F, N
Rowan *(Sorbus aucuparia)* F
Whitebeam *(Sorbus aria)* F
Hawthorn *(Crataegus monogyna)* F, N
Holly *(Ilex aquifolium)* F, C
Hazel *(Corylus avellana)* N, F
Guelder rose *(Viburnum opulus)* F
Dog rose *(Rosa canina)* F, N
Dogwood *(Cornus sanguinea)* I

RECOMMENDED WOODLAND FLOWERS

Common dog violet
(Viola riviniana) N
Foxglove *(Digitalis purpurea)* B
Lesser celandine
(Ranunculus ficaria)
Lily of the valley
(Convallaria majalis)
Primrose *(Primula vulgaris)* N
Stinking hellebore
(Helleborus foetidus) B
Wood anemone
(Anemone nemorosa)
Wood crane's-bill
(Geranium sylvaticum)
Wood forget-me-not
(Myosotis sylvatica) B

NOVEMBER

This month is the start of the bird-feeding season and there will be a noticeable return to the garden of resident species which have been feeding further afield. The cold weather can also drive whole flocks or migrants to seek shelter in towns, including large numbers of chaffinches and blackbirds from northern Scandinavia, where winter comes early. The best food source is the long-lasting berries on cotoneaster, pyracantha, berberis and holly but these can disappear literally overnight if a migrating flock of fieldfares descends. Once the natural resources have gone, it is time to dust off the bird table and start winter feeding.

Traditionally, this is bonfire month and whilst there is nothing like the smell of woodsmoke, there are more constructive things to be done with garden rubbish. Compost heaps come in to their own now, providing a way of recycling garden waste and providing homes for slow worms, toads, shrews and wood mice.

The hedgerows are full of native plants in fruit, with many rosehips and berries still intact. Most noticeable this month is the old man's beard or wild clematis, whose fluffy white seedheads may be seen alongside the white globular fruits of the snowberry – an American plant which has become naturalised in Britain.

For the wildlife gardener, the usual tasks of clearing up, cutting back and tidying up the garden should really give way to jobs that will help the resident wildlife make it through the winter ahead. By removing all traces of fallen leaves and dying plants we are taking away vital warmth, food and protective cover for a whole range of insects, birds and mammals. Leave the garden to die back naturally and the creatures in it will have a better chance of surviving until spring.

tasks
FOR THE
month

BULB PLANTING 2

The second phase of bulb planting can take place this month. Snakeshead fritillary *(Fritillaria meleagris)* should be given a place in short grass or on damp soil where it will flower in mid- or late spring. Tulips can also be planted now, and will thrive in pots, beds or rockeries. The highly bred garden forms are not as good for insects as the wild tulip *(Tulipa sylvestris)*, which grows naturally under hedges and in woodlands, and flowers in mid-spring. Summer-flowering lilies can be planted in an open position with good drainage. There are hundreds of exotic varieties available, but two naturalised species are the tall, pink martagon lily *(Lilium martagon)* and the yellow Pyrenean lily *(Lilium pyrenaicum)*. Both are easy to establish and rich in nectar.

DEALING WITH AUTUMN LEAVES

A layer of fallen leaves in a woodland area will break down into an ideal growing medium for trees and should not be removed. However it is sensible to rake or sweep up leaves from paths and grassy areas. There are two useful ways of using the collected leaves. The simplest method is just to pile them under hedges or in a spare corner, where they will provide cover for spiders and a host of insects which in turn will provide food for robins and wrens. Piles of leaves are also useful for hibernating hedgehogs. Alternatively, large quantities of leaves can be converted into leaf mould to use as a mulch or to dig into the soil to improve its condition.

Making leaf mould
■ Collect leaves with a spring-tined rake or broom – oak and beech make very good leaf mould but any deciduous leaves will do.

■ Pile the leaves into an unused corner of the garden or into a wire netting container. A simple container can be made by driving a single 90cm (3ft) post into the ground and attaching netting in a cylinder shape around it.

■ Firm the leaves down as they accumulate – if they are particularly dry, water the pile with a watering-can.

■ Leave the pile undisturbed for a year, when it will have produced good crumbly leaf mould.

A SIMPLE WIRE-NETTING LEAF MOULD CONTAINER

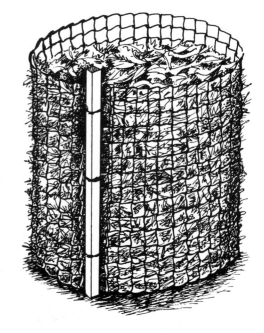

Keeping the pond free of leaves

It is better to fish out fallen leaves with a long-handled net than to cover the whole pond with netting. Frogs and toads still need to be able to get in and out and birds to drink and bathe. A few leaves will just decompose and add to the material in the pond, but large quantities from overhanging trees should be removed.

BONFIRES

As far as wildlife is concerned, bonfires are bad news. Every year, thousands of hedgehogs and small mammals meet their death by climbing into inviting-looking piles of wood, hoping for an undisturbed hibernation. The tradition of burning garden prunings and clippings is a great waste of potential sites for overwintering insects, like harvestmen, who actually help gardeners by eating smaller flying insects. The whole concept of 'rubbish' in a garden needs to undergo a rethink. Decaying plant material is vital to the natural cycle of growth and we should resist the temptation to tidy or clean up the garden too meticulously. Starting a compost heap, or simply piling unwanted wood and vegetation in a corner is a far better use of the garden's resources.

THE FLOWER BED

Borders do tend to look rather tatty at this time of year with few if any flowers, yellowing or fallen leaves and broken stems. The good news is you don't need to do anything about it. Those hollow stems and empty seed pods are providing homes for ladybirds, which if you nurture them over the winter will be ready to feed on the first batch of aphids as they emerge in the spring.

MAKING WINTER HABITATS

Apart from the habitats created by the untidy flower border or hedge bottom, it is possible to create · additional overwintering sites specifically to attract wildlife. Choose a corner of the garden which is rarely used, behind a shed or some fairly inaccessible spot which can remain undisturbed for years if necessary. This rough corner should be well away from the house, so that disturbance is kept to a minimum. It also ensures that unwanted wildlife like field mice are not tempted too close to the house (see pp80-1 – Establishing an Untidy Area).

■ A pile of logs or old timber will soon be covered in fungi, and offer shelter to hedgehogs, wood mice, wrens and possibly foxes.

■ A pile of rocks, stones or old paving slabs will harbour insects, possibly slow worms, and offer shelter to hibernating frogs and toads.

■ Loosely piled grass clippings or straw will also house insects and ground-feeding birds. They may also attract field mice and shrews.

■ A sheet of corrugated iron is an ideal habitat for many types of reptiles and small mammals who will use the 'tunnels' as convenient hiding places.

CUTTING BACK IVY

Mature ivy plants, trained against a house or shed wall can become overgrown and start to block gutters and downpipes. If this is the case, it can be cut back towards the end of this month, once flowering has finished. Cut all stems to a level 90cm (3ft) below the gutters and gently pull away the excess growth.

Fritillaria

USE LEAVES FOR COMPOST
If there are not enough leaves in the garden to make leaf mould, they can be added to the compost heap.

plants
OF THE
month

GARDEN CLEMATIS
In addition to the native clematis,
C. montana *is worth including in*
the wildlife garden. Its vigorous
growth can cover a trellis in a
single season and will soon
produce a dense tangle of stems
for nesting birds.

BARBERRY
(Berberis thunbergii)

One of a whole group of garden shrubs that bears berries well into winter. Not a native plant but a valuable addition to the wildlife garden.

type	Deciduous shrub
flowers	Pale yellow, spring
fruits	Scarlet berries from mid-autumn to mid-winter
height	1.2m (4ft)
spread	2m (6ft)
planting	Plant young specimens between mid-autumn and early spring. For hedging, plants should be set 0.5m (1ft 8in) apart
site	In a sunny position in the shrub border or to form a hedge
soil	Any. Tolerates poor, shallow soils
care	No regular pruning required. Old plants should have woody stems cut out at ground level in late winter. Hedges can be trimmed if necessary in late summer or early autumn
propagation	From semi-hardwood cuttings in late summer
related species	The slightly larger *Berberis aggregata* is another good species to look out for. In particular *B. aggregata* 'Barbarossa' is heavily laden with coral-red berries at this time of year
wildlife value	The mass of small berries can be relied upon to last through the worst part of the winter, providing food for resident and visiting birds. The spiny leaves also give good protection for nesting in spring and summer

FIRETHORN
(Pyracantha)

Pyracantha is an excellent autumn shrub for its bright berries, but also produces delicate hawthorn-like blossom in early summer. It forms a loosely shaped, informal bush which can be trained on a trellis or wires to grow against a wall.

type	Evergreen shrub
flowers	White, early summer
fruits/berries	Orange-red, mid-autumn to late winter
height	2.5m (8ft)
spread	3m (10ft)
planting	Plant young plants from mid-autumn to early spring
site	Full sun or shade, will tolerate a north- or east-facing wall
soil	Fertile, well-drained soil
care	If grown as a free-standing shrub, no pruning is necessary. Any excessive growth on wall-trained plants can be trimmed back after flowering
propagation	From semi-hardwood cuttings taken in late summer
varieties	*P.* 'Orange Glow' is a very vigorous hybrid. *P. crenulata* 'Flava' has bright yellow berries
wildlife value	Long-lasting berries provide food for the birds on a first-come, first-served basis. The frothy flowers are also popular with foraging insects

OLD MAN'S BEARD
(Clematis vitalba)

The wild scrambling clematis gets its name quite obviously from the white, billowing masses that hold the seedheads. It also goes by the name of traveller's joy, perhaps because of its fast-growing habit, or perhaps because of its tendency to colonise railway embankments, where the fluffy seedheads can be seen by travellers. It is really too rampant for the garden proper, but it is useful for covering unwanted sheds or outbuildings and looks magnificent scrambling through a native hedge.

type	Deciduous climber
seedheads	White, feathery masses, mid-autumn to early winter
flowers	Green-white, mid-summer to early autumn
height	15m (50ft). Will grow upwards if supported by a tall tree or shrub, but tends to scramble horizontally
planting	Put in new plants between mid-autumn and early spring
site	Plant next to wall or fence, within an existing hedge or train up through a dead tree. Any aspect. Give new plants some support with wire netting or trellis
soil	Prefers chalk soils
care	If plant outgrows its space, cut back shoots by two-thirds in late winter
propagation	From semi-hardwood cuttings taken in late summer
wildlife value	The heavily scented flowers are an excellent nectar source for night-hunting moths, hoverflies and bees. Seedheads are popular with birds

GUELDER ROSE
(Viburnum opulus)

Grown mainly for its brilliant berries, the guelder rose is one of the best native shrubs for creating an informal hedge or woodland-edge habitat. In the wild, it can be found in damp woodlands.

type	Deciduous shrub
flowers	Creamy white, early summer
fruits	Clusters of translucent scarlet-red berries, mid-autumn to early winter
height	4m (12ft)
spread	3–4m (10–12ft)
planting	Plant young trees between mid-autumn and early spring
site	Partial or full shade, in shrub border or woodland edge
soil	Rich, moist soil
care	No regular pruning required, but dead wood can be thinned out from overgrown shrubs after flowering
propagation	From semi-hardwood cuttings taken in late summer
varieties	*V. opulus* 'Compactum' is a better choice for small gardens, reaching only 1.8m (6ft) high
wildlife value	The berries provide a good early winter food source for birds and the flowers are particularly attractive to hoverflies

THE WAYFARING TREE
A close relative of the guelder rose, the wayfaring tree (Viburnum lantana) has similar flowers but the berries turn black when fully ripe. It forms a small tree rather than a shrub and is equally popular with birds and insects.

GUELDER ROSE

practical project

STARTING A COMPOST HEAP

WHERE TO SITE THE HEAP
The compost bin or heap should be out of direct sunlight (to prevent it drying out too quickly). Site it away from overhanging trees, which would drip water directly onto the compost. Place it on earth or grass – not concrete – so that worms and insects can enter from the bottom. If possible, raise it slightly off the ground with bricks or wood to allow the air to circulate underneath.

Autumn is a logical time of year to start a compost heap, simply because there are lots of prunings and cuttings available, although in fact it can be started at any time of year. A good compost heap has a dual purpose, providing excellent organic matter for the garden and an extra habitat for wildlife.

BIN OR HEAP?

As far as the actual compost is concerned it does not really matter if you use a bin or just make a pile in a corner of the garden. The simplest type of heap is a pyramid shape of material, topped with a piece of old carpet. For a tidier effect, there are several sorts of square bin available made from wire netting or wooden planks. These are preferable to the plastic containers and tumblers which do not allow access to wildlife. One of the simplest and most successful designs is the wooden slatted 'box' made from spaced planks of wood which allows birds and toads to get to

WARNING

■ *It is best to avoid cooked food scraps or animal products which may attract rats* ■

the insects within the compost. Whichever type you choose, make sure it is at least 90cm (3ft) square or bigger, if space allows. Ideally, have two bins, side by side. This makes turning easier, as the material from one can be turned into the other. Alternatively, one can be filled and left to mature whilst the other is being filled with fresh material.

MAKING COMPOST

There are three essentials for making good compost: air, water and nitrogen.

■ *Air* needs to be able to circulate around the heap and within it – the secret is not to pack down the material too firmly.

■ *Water* The heap should be moist, but not sodden. If the material is dry it should be sprinkled with water occasionally. A 'lid' of old carpet, thick newspapers or polythene will help to keep out any really heavy downpours.

■ *Nitrogen* is the activator that speeds up the decaying process. Any material rich in nitrogen will do: poultry manure, fresh nettles, stable manure, liquid seaweed – even human urine.

AN EFFECTIVE WOODEN COMPOST BIN DESIGN

Two bins side by side is the ideal arrangement

Composting method

■ Collect enough material to fill the bin at least half full. If necessary, store in plastic sacks until you have enough. Add the material to the bin in layers of about 15cm (6in). Put the activating material between each layer.

■ Continue adding material until the bin is full. Avoid adding too much of any one type of material and put the 'lid' back on each time to keep in the heat.

■ After about six weeks the compost heap can be turned. Using a fork, turn the material over (into an adjoining bin, if possible), making sure any dry woody material at the edges is brought into the centre. However, if you want to be sure not to disturb any nesting or hibernating wildlife, it is better to leave it unturned. It will still make good compost but it may take a little longer.

■ Sit back and wait. Good compost takes around six months to mature (8–12 months unturned). Meanwhile, start a second heap.

WHAT HAPPENS INSIDE A COMPOST HEAP

The first things to be broken down are the soft plant leaves and stems – bacteria work on their sugars and produce heat. In the first week the interior of the heap reaches a high temperature, destroying pests and weed seeds and causing the heap to 'steam' on a cold morning. Next the fungi start to work, breaking down the raw material. If you pull back the lid after a couple of weeks you may see the white mycelia of the fungi, lacing their way across the heap. A whole range of microscopic organisms and larger insects now appear, such as spring tails which feed on the fungi and are, in turn, eaten by beetles. Snails, slugs, centipedes, spiders, mites, and eelworms move in and the whole heap becomes a rich feeding ground for frogs, toads, birds and hedgehogs.

WILDLIFE AND THE COMPOST HEAP

Apart from being a food source for wildlife, the heat and moisture provided by the heap make it attractive for nesting. Slow-worms have been known to lay their young in the warmth of the heap and grass snakes may lay their clutch of eggs in an undisturbed heap during summer, the young hatching out in early autumn. Hedgehogs do not normally hibernate in compost, as they prefer a drier site. However, they may well 'live' there throughout the summer with a steady supply of slugs on hand. Frogs, toads and newts may utilise the moisture of the heap for hibernation, and toads particularly will not stray far from a good heap all year round.

USING COMPOST

If you decide not to turn the heap, the compost you produce may be a little coarser than the product of a regularly turned heap. It may not be fine enough to use for seed growing and potting, but it will still make an excellent material for planting new shrubs and trees, to dig into the garden as a soil improver, or to use as a mulch.

COMPOST MATERIALS TO AVOID

■ *Diseased plants* should be burnt. The ash can be added to the heap

■ *Perennial weeds and their roots*, particularly ground elder and dandelions

■ *Cooked food*

■ *Too many grass clippings.* Only add in shallow layers

■ *Woody material that has not been cut into smaller pieces*

WHAT WENT WRONG

■ *Compost too slimy* The material is either getting too wet or contains too many grass cuttings. As a general rule, no more than a third of the compost should be grass cuttings.

■ *Compost too dry and woody* The material has not been chopped up small enough and contains too much wood from shrubs and trees. Add shallow layers of softer matter (such as some vegetable peelings and grass cuttings) and an 'activator' such as nettles or stable manure.

COMPOST MATERIALS

Dead flowers, bedding plants, plant stems

Lawn clippings (*in small quantities*)

Leaves (*in small quantities – large quantities should be piled separately to make leaf mould*)

Newspapers (*shredded and moistened*)

Pondweed

Prunings from trees and shrubs (*only if finely shredded*)

Raw vegetable matter (*potato peelings, rotten fruit, sprout stalks etc*)

Straw (*including bedding from caged pets*)

Tea bags or tea leaves

Weeds (*all except problem perennial weeds like ground elder*)

DECEMBER

This is the traditional time for plants like holly, mistletoe and ivy which carry their own seasonal associations and are steeped in folklore. Holly is said to have power over evil forces and also to protect and provide. This it certainly does – witness the number of creatures seeking out the bush for shelter and food. Ivy is the symbol of everlasting life and friendship. Considering how it continues to cling and climb and provide greenery in every season, it is hard to imagine a more trustworthy garden plant. Mistletoe, on the other hand, is often feared by gardeners as a parasite and destroyer of trees. In fact, although it draws minerals from its host tree, it does not cause serious damage and there are records of mistletoe growing on oak trees for a hundred years or more. With the first really hard frost of winter, the wildlife garden turns into a sanctuary for foraging birds. The familiar sparrows, robins and blackbirds will be joined by pied wagtails driven in from open parkland and fields, wood pigeons and feral pigeons in search of extra food, as well as continental visitors like blackcaps, redwings, fieldfares and siskins. Wrens, thrushes, dunnocks and tits may all utilise the food and water a garden provides.

Many native mammals are still active in the woods and hedgerows. Foxes will be seeking out food during a cold spell and may visit gardens under cover of darkness. For others, the month is spent underground, like the badgers who line their setts in the autumn and venture out less and less as the weather gets colder. With the last of the deciduous leaves blown to earth, the bones of the wildlife garden are laid bare, revealing shapes it was impossible to see amongst the luxuriant growth of spring and summer. On a frosty day under blue skies, a walk around the garden is one of the most refreshing and enjoyable ways to end the year.

tasks

FOR THE

month

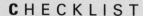

CHECKLIST

- Start feeding birds
- Keep pond free of ice
- Plant bare-root roses
- Coppice trees and shrubs

BIRD FEEDING

Start to put out food for the birds this month. There should still be some natural food available in the form of berries, but flower seeds and windfallen fruit are finished. Regular feeding encourages birds to get into the habit of visiting the bird table, which means they are more likely to survive the winter and use the garden to breed in the spring. Unsalted nuts, seeds, dried fruit, grated cheese and apples are all acceptable foods. (See pp132-3 for advice on choosing bird tables and feeders.)

KEEPING POND FREE OF ICE

The weather this month is often not as harsh as expected. However, if a freeze does come, it is important to keep ponds and water sources free of ice and easily available to wildlife. (See p13 for methods.)

PLANTING BARE-ROOT SHRUB ROSES

If the weather is still frost free, bare-root shrub roses ordered from nurseries can be planted this month. The planting method applies to: *Rosa rugosa*, *Rosa canina*, *Rosa rubiginosa* and *Rosa glauca*. If the ground is frozen it is better to wait until late winter or early spring.

NOTE

- *Container-grown roses from garden centres can be planted at any time of year as long as the ground is not frozen or waterlogged* ▪

Plant the roses as soon as possible after they arrive. If this is not possible, the roots should be buried in a shallow trench in the garden and watered. They can be left for several months like this before replanting.

Shrub roses should be planted 1.5m (5ft) away from the next shrub.

▪ Using secateurs, cut off any leaves, flower buds or damaged stems (make any cuts to an outward-facing bud).

▪ Dig a hole to fit the shape of the roots – usually this is no more than 25cm (10in) deep, but may be up to 60cm (2ft) across.

▪ Mix some of the soil from the hole with organic manure or garden compost and spread a 5cm (2in) layer of the mixture at the bottom of the hole.

▪ Spread out the roots in the hole, adjusting the planting depth, if necessary, to ensure that the junction between the rootstock and the stem will be level with the surrounding soil. Fill with ordinary soil and tread lightly, adding a final layer of soil as needed.

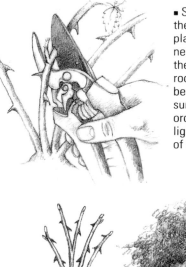

Coppicing

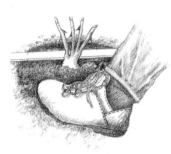

> **NOTE**
>
> ■ *Shrub roses may be pruned in the first spring after planting* ■

●

COPPICING TREES AND SHRUBS

The ancient skill of coppicing has been practised at least since Anglo-Saxon times and possibly longer. As a traditional form of woodland management, it served two important functions: to provide a renewable source of wood for fuel and fencing and to allow selected trees space to grow to full maturity for subsequent cropping as timber. It also had a secondary (probably unintentional) effect which was to let in light to the woodland floor, regenerating the plants and flowers growing there, and their dependent wildlife. Coppice shoots also provided food for deer, which may or may not have been welcome depending on the purpose of the wood. The word 'copse' denotes a wood that was once coppiced.

It is not necessary to have acres of land or a full-blown wood to practise coppicing in the garden. In fact, if space is restricted, coppicing native shrubs and trees allows gardeners to grow a greater range of species than there would normally be room for.

What is coppicing?

Coppicing means cutting the tree down to ground level, to allow new shoots to spring up from the base. Far from killing the tree, this practice encourages the tree's natural power of regeneration, whereby it will throw up new poles of wood, year after year.

Why coppice?

A coppiced woodland, even on a small scale, allows a broad range of plants, birds, mammals and insects to co-exist. The main, tall-growing trees such as oak, beech and ash provide the upper canopy for nesting birds. This is underplanted with a layer of smaller trees and shrubs which may be coppiced; white willow, wych-elm, hornbeam, bird cherry, hazel and lime. Beneath this, on the woodland floor, primroses, bluebells and other woodland plants flourish in the leaf mould and dappled shade provided by the trees above.

In the garden, coppiced trees will not produce blossom or berries, but the young leaves and shoots produced in the spring will support a new generation of butterfly caterpillars and other leaf-eating insects.

How to coppice

■ *Year 1*
Use pruners for small stems and a strong pruning saw for thicker ones. Cut the stems to a few inches above ground level.

■ *Subsequent years*
Depending on how fast the different species grow, some coppicing can take place every winter. It is usual to rotate the cropping, so that there is a succession of available wood. Each individual tree or shrub should be left between five and seven years before coppicing again, allowing it to form a medium-sized shrub. If the wood is not needed for a specific purpose, trees and shrubs may be coppiced whenever they outgrow their allotted space.

■ As the years go by, a coppiced tree will start to form a stool. Shoots thrown up from this stool should be cut back to within 5–8cm (2–3in) of this old wood.

●

POLLARDING

Pollarding is another traditional method of restricting the size of trees and letting more light reach the ground. Instead of cutting the stems to ground level, the trunk is cut at a height of 2–5m (6–15ft) leaving a permanent trunk called a 'bolling'. New shoots then sprout from the bolling, keeping the wood out of reach of animals until it is cut for use. It is best to select a young tree for pollarding, before the trunk is too large – older trees need to be done professionally. Pollarding is usually carried out on isolated trees, or those in formal rows, not those in the centre of a wood where it would be difficult to work. Poles of wood can be cut from the tree every year, but re-pollarding should only take place every ten to twenty years.

SHRUBS AND TREES SUITABLE FOR COPPICING

Ash (*Fraxinus excelsior*)
Common alder (*Alnus glutinosa*)
Downy birch (*Betula pubescens*)
Elder (*Sambucus nigra*)
Field maple (*Acer campestre*)
Goat willow (*Salix caprea*)
Hazel (*Corylus avellana*)
Holly (*Ilex aquifolium*)
Hornbeam (*Carpinus betulus*)
Oak (*Quercus robur*)
Silver birch (*Betula pendula*)
Small-leaved lime (*Tilia cordata*)
White willow (*Salix alba*)
Wych elm (*Ulmus glabra*)

USING COPPICED WOOD
The poles make good firewood, but they are also extremely useful for fence posts, tree stakes, hurdle making and wattle work.

Pollarding

plants
OF THE
month

care After planting keep well watered, especially through the summer. Pinch out the shoots of new hedging in the first spring after planting. When fully grown, trim hedges annually in early spring (after berries are finished but before nesting begins). Trees do not need regular pruning

propagation By cuttings taken in late summer

varieties *I. aquifolium* 'J. C. van Tol' and 'Pyramidalis' will bear berries without a nearby male tree. *I. aquifolium* 'Argentea Marginata' has a heavy crop of berries and silver-edged leaves

wildlife value One of the best trees for nesting birds, because of the protection against predators offered by the spiny leaves. The berries last well into the coldest part of winter, providing food for resident birds and particularly for visiting fieldfares and redwings

HOLLY
(Ilex aquifolium)

The so-called English holly is native to most parts of Britain and literally hundreds of varieties can be found growing in gardens, parks and in the countryside. An excellent wildlife tree to plant on the edge of the woodland or as a boundary hedge.

type Evergreen tree
flowers White, spring
fruits Bright red berries from late autumn to late winter are usually borne on female trees, and there needs to be a male tree nearby to ensure fertilisation
height 5–8m (15–25ft)
spread 2.5–4m (8–13ft)
planting Plant young specimens in autumn or any time during the winter if the ground is not frozen. Add some garden compost or manure to the planting hole. For hedging, choose plants about 45cm (18in) high and space them at 60cm (24in) intervals
site Sun or shade. Variegated forms will have better colouring in a sunny position. Very tolerant of pollution and salt spray; useful for screening in coastal or built-up areas
soil Any

HAWTHORN
(Crataegus monogyna)

Also known as May blossom, the common hawthorn is a much-loved native shrub. In the wild it grows profusely in woodland and scrub, on heaths and in hedgerows, where its clouds of blossom used to correspond with May Day in the old calendar. In late autumn and winter, the scarlet berries mark the passing of the seasons; when the hawthorn berries have disappeared it is time to get out the bird table.

MIDLAND HAWTHORN
The Midland hawthorn (Crataegus laevigata) is somewhat smaller than the common hawthorn, reaching only 5m (15ft), and a good choice where space is limited. The flowers are purely white and scented and it can be distinguished from C. monogyna by the berries, which have two or three pips instead of one.

type	Deciduous shrub or tree
flowers	White, sometimes tinged pink, early summer
fruits	Red berries, mid-autumn to early winter
height	Up to 8m (25ft)
spread	5m (15ft)
planting	Plant young trees between mid-autumn and early spring when the ground is workable. For a hedge, use plants 45cm (18in) high and space them 30cm (12in) apart
site	Sun or partial shade. As a screen, hedge or planted at the edge of a woodland belt
soil	Any
care	No regular pruning required, although trees that get too large can be cut back hard in mid-summer. Trim hedges annually, after flowering and after any nesting birds have vacated the hedge – it is usually safe to do so by late summer or early autumn
propagation	From seed sown in autumn
varieties	*C. monogyna* 'Biflora' is an unusual variety that produces flowers and leaves from mid-autumn to early spring in mild winters. It is also known as the Glastonbury Thorn – legend has it that on a visit to Glastonbury one Christmas Day, Joseph of Arimathea drove his staff into the ground and *C. monogyna* 'Biflora' burst into flower
wildlife value	The berries are a useful food source for birds in late autumn and winter. The dense tangle of thorns makes an excellent nesting site in spring and, in early summer, the sweetly scented blossom is very attractive to a whole range of insects. There are over a hundred insect species specifically associated with hawthorn

MISTLETOE
(*Viscum album*)

This native plant is found growing on the branches of deciduous trees, especially apples, poplars, willows, limes and sometimes oaks. It is usually planted by birds feeding on the berries and wiping their beaks against the bark of nearby trees.

type	Evergreen, parasitic shrub
flowers	Yellow-green, late winter to mid-spring
fruits	Semi-translucent white berries, mid-autumn to mid-winter
spread	Clumps up to 60cm (2ft) across
propagation	In mid-winter take berries from a tree in the garden or in the wild. (Don't use shop-bought sprigs which may be imported species, not suited to growing in Britain.) Push the berries under a flap of cut bark or into existing crevices. It is best to try this on a tree of the same type from which the parent plant was taken. Germination will take three months and berries will not appear on the new plant for seven years
wildlife value	The white, globular berries are a good food source for birds. The sticky pulp surrounding the seeds sticks to their beaks and in an endeavour to remove it, the seeds are wiped onto the trunk of the next tree, getting trapped in the grooves of the bark

WINTER CELEBRATIONS
Evergreens have special significance at this time of year, retaining their foliage and colour when other plants are losing theirs. Ivy, holly and mistletoe bear fruit in the dead of winter – a good reason to share the bounty with the garden's creatures. Bring boughs of holly and mistletoe into the house for the festive season, and afterwards put them into a corner of the garden to wither naturally. Blackbirds, thrushes and ground-feeding wrens will pick off any left-over berries.

practical project

CHOOSING A BIRD TABLE OR FEEDER

There is a bewildering choice of bird tables and feeders available from garden centres and by mail order. Some are very high-tech in design, with shoots, perches, roofs and ledges in chrome and plastic. These seem rather elaborate for what is basically a straightforward job – presenting food to the birds in a place where they can eat safely and where humans can watch them do so. In fact, research shows that birds are completely indifferent to what the table or feeder looks like, as long as they can reach the food safely and easily.

The simple, traditional wooden bird table is still a favourite for a natural-looking garden but, to be functional, it should incorporate certain basic features. A raised rim around the edge of the tray is useful to prevent food from being knocked off, and there should be a small gap in this rim to allow rainwater to drain away. The base must be sturdy enough to stop it being knocked over by pets, children, or indeed foxes searching for food. A roof is not essential but it does keep the food dry and protected from snow falls.

HANGING FEEDERS

These feeders are designed to be hung from the table, or from a window ledge, wall, or fence. Many birds prefer this kind of acrobatic feeding, particularly tits, finches and even sparrows.

Feeders containing nuts are usually cylinders of wire mesh, plastic mesh bags or metal spirals. Models with a spring-action bottom plate are a good idea, as it prevents nuts becoming trapped at the bottom and left to rot. If your model does not have this feature, make sure you periodically take down the feeder and scrape out any old nuts that have become stuck to the bottom.

WINDOW FEEDERS

A feeder that fixes directly to the window is one of the best ways to see birds at close quarters. These devices are especially useful for people who are housebound, but also practical for flat dwellers with no access to a garden. Again there are many designs available, but a simple one made of clear plastic that sticks to the window with suckers is probably as good as any.

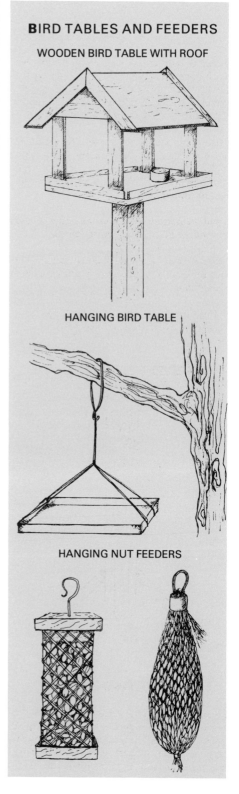

BIRD TABLES AND FEEDERS

WOODEN BIRD TABLE WITH ROOF

HANGING BIRD TABLE

HANGING NUT FEEDERS

DIY TABLE

Detailed instructions for making bird tables can be obtained from the Royal Society for the Protection of Birds (address on p141). However, a basic table is easy and cheap to make if you follow the instructions below.

- Use an old wooden tray with a lip around it and nail it to a stout post about 1.2m–1.5m (4–5 ft) high. A good straight length of tree branch will work just as well as specially bought timber.

- Nail the bottom of the post to a large square of wood, to give the structure stability.

- Add pieces of wood of equal length and with their ends cut at angles around the base of the table.

- Position the table on level ground, weighting it with stones if necessary.

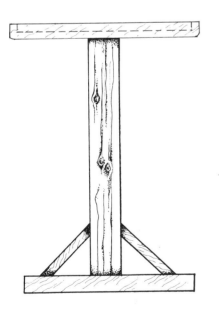

WHO FEEDS WHERE

To ensure that all the birds in the garden are catered for, it is a good idea to have three types of feeding situation: a table, several hanging feeders, and also food on the ground. (For more details on what to feed, see p12.)

Table-feeding birds
Robins, house sparrows, tree sparrows, collared doves, chaffinches, bramblings, wood pigeons, bullfinches, greenfinches.

Acrobatic-feeding birds
Blue tits, great tits, coal tits, siskins, nuthatches, house sparrows, tree sparrows, bullfinches, greenfinches.

Ground-feeding birds
Blackbirds, thrushes, dunnocks, wrens, fieldfares, redwings.

WHERE TO SITE THE BIRD TABLE

The feeding area should be in clear view of one or more windows in the house, where everyone can see it. Birds seem to get used to human activity so it can be placed quite close to the house. Make sure it is a couple of metres (a few feet) away from dense cover, where cats or other predators could hide.

WARNING

- *Cats are one of the most distressing predators in suburban gardens. A cat will not usually jump 1.5m (5ft) into the air and on to the table unless there is a convenient jumping-off point, but it may well try to climb the bird-table post. One form of deterrent is a metal cone attached to the post, two-thirds of the way up. An inverted biscuit tin works just as well. It may also deter squirrels from stealing the food, although they are incredibly agile and may not be so easily put off* ∎

ATTRACTING WOODPECKERS

Making a Log Feeder
Woodpeckers are frequently seen in gardens, pecking away in the crevices in tree bark for their insect food. Take a piece of rotten log, make a few deep holes in the wood and stuff them full of lard or suet, mixed with bird seed. Suspend the log from the branch of a tree to attract both greater and lesser spotted woodpeckers. Incidentally, the green woodpecker spends more time on the ground than other woodpeckers and may not feed on the log.

plants
OF THE
month

COTONEASTER

Most of the cotoneasters grown in Britain are not native species, but introductions from China and the Himalayas. There is a very rare wild cotoneaster (C. integerriumus) which although found widely in Europe occurs in only one or two sites in Britain. However the garden varieties are excellent for birds and offer a range of potential uses to the wildlife gardener.

COTONEASTER SPECIES
C. dammeri

type	Evergreen
flowers	White, early summer
fruits	Red berries, mid-autumn to mid-winter
height	5–8cm (2–3in)
spread	1.8m (6ft)
habit	Low growing
uses	Ground cover, banks, beneath trees and shrubs
wildlife value	Berries for ground-feeding birds like blackbirds and cover for insects such as slugs and ground beetles, which in turn are eaten by the birds

C. horizontalis

type	Deciduous shrub
flowers	Pink, early summer
fruits	Red berries, mid-autumn to mid-winter
height	60cm (2ft)
spread	1.8m (6ft)
habit	Horizontally spreading
uses	To grow against a north or east-facing wall, to cover unsightly banks or bare rocks
wildlife value	Berries are highly sought after by birds and the foliage provides good nesting cover when grown against a wall

C. microphyllus

type	Dwarf evergreen shrub
flowers	White, late spring, early summer
fruits	Scarlet berries, mid-autumn to early winter
height	15cm (6in)
spread	1.8m (6ft)
habit	Low growing, spreading
uses	Edging flower beds, ground cover, banks, low walls
wildlife value	Cover and insects for ground-feeding birds like wrens, plus berries in autumn and early winter

C. simonsii

type	Evergreen shrub
flowers	White, early summer
fruits	Orange-red berries, mid-autumn to early winter
height	1.8m (6ft)
spread	1.5m (5ft)
habit	Erect
uses	Hedging, either on its own or as part of a mixed hedge
wildlife value	A hedge of *C. simonsii* serves a dual purpose: a secure nesting site in the spring and food in the autumn and early winter

CAUTION
Although good for birds to eat, all parts of the cotoneaster shrub, including the berries, are mildly poisonous. If eaten, they can cause digestive upsets.

COTONEASTER FRIGIDUS

C. frigidus

type	Semi-evergreen tree/shrub
flowers	White, early summer
fruits	Red berries, mid-autumn to mid-winter
height	4m (13ft)
spread	3m (10ft)
habit	Small tree or shrub
uses	As a specimen tree or part of a shrub border
wildlife value	Large, heavy bunches of berries are very popular with birds, especially waxwings

CULTIVATION
of cotoneasters

site	Sunny
soil	Ordinary garden soil

planting	Between mid-summer and late winter. Hedging plants like *C. simonsii* should be placed at 30cm (12in) intervals
care	After planting, remove the tips of the shoots to encourage bushy growth. No regular pruning is required, but if plants are old or overgrown, cut back deciduous types in late winter, evergreens in mid-spring. Evergreen hedges do usually need pruning each year – cut out vigorous new shoots and side shoots immediately after flowering.
propagation	Propagation is by semi-hardwood cuttings taken in late summer.

appendix
1

CONTAINER
GARDENING FOR
WILDLIFE

It is quite possible to entice wildlife into even the most unpromising paved areas by utilising containers. Several mini-habitats can be created by growing a carefully selected range of trees, shrubs and flowers in pots, tubs, window boxes and hanging baskets.

If the space is enclosed by walls or high fences, it is important to let the passing wildlife know that this area is a source of food and shelter. Aim to add height and greenery with a small native tree grown in a good-sized wooden barrel and add one or two berry-bearing shrubs. Clothe the walls in climbers for nesting birds and introduce nectar-rich flowers for the insects. Finally, put up a nesting box amongst the climbers and find a place for a feeding table in winter and a bird bath in summer. Despite the lack of grass and full-size trees, a surprising range of creatures will begin to inhabit this new garden.

DON'T FORGET HERBS

Herbs are amongst the most useful wildlife plants, including borage, mint, chives and rosemary, and are ideally suited to container growing. Do allow them to flower though, even at the expense of a continuous supply of leaves for cooking.

FOUR-SEASON
WINDOW BOX

Try planting a window box with the following selection of evergreens, perennials, bulbs and bedding plants, for an all-the-year-round display.

WINTER

Ivy, hellebores, snowdrops

SPRING

Ivy, yellow crocus and grape hyacinths

SUMMER

Ivy, white alyssum and dwarf lavender

AUTUMN

Ivy, meadow saffron

DON'T FORGET WATER
Don't forget water for a container garden; a large plant saucer will do as a source of water for wildlife, or make use of an old sink, plastic tub or washing up bowl as a bird bath.

STEP-BY-STEP CONTAINER PLANTING

■ Make sure the container has adequate drainage holes and that they are free of obstruction.

■ Put a layer of broken clay pots or crockery over the base of the container.

■ Half fill with a multi-purpose potting compost.

■ Place the plants in position and fill around the root ball with more compost. Press down firmly.

■ Water well and add more compost if necessary, to bring the level to 2.5cm (1in) below the rim of the container.

PLAN OF A SMALL ENCLOSED PATIO WITH CONTAINERS

RECOMMENDED PLANTS

TREES
Rowan (*Sorbus aucuparia* 'Fastigiata')
Dwarf form (3m/10ft). Flowers for insects and berries for birds.

Willow (*Salix caprea* 'Pendula')
Weeping form (3m/10ft). Catkins for insects, young leaves for caterpillars.

SHRUBS
Buddleia davidii
(3m/10ft) nectar flowers for butterflies.

***Cotoneaster* 'Hybridus Pendulus'**
(3m/10ft) berries and flowers.

Hawthorn (*Crataegus monogyna*)
(5m/15ft) can be pruned hard to keep it within bounds. Secure nesting site for birds. Berries and flowers.

Holly (*Ilex aquifolium*)
(To 5m/15ft) a male and female bush are needed to be sure of berries. Nesting cover for birds.

Lavender (*Lavandula angustifolia*)
Scented bee flowers.

CLIMBERS
Honeysuckle (*Lonicera periclymenum*)
Summer wall and fence cover. Nectar flowers.

Ivy (*Hedera helix*)
All-year-round wall and fence cover. Nectar flowers.

FLOWERS FOR NECTAR
Alyssum
Candytuft (*Iberis*)
Nasturtium (*Tropaeolum majus*)
Nicotiana
Night-scented stock (*Matthiola bicornis*)
Pot marigold (*Calendula officinalis*)

NOTE

■ To boost the wildlife habitat in a concrete yard, make a pile of logs in one corner. As the wood begins to break down, it will house beetles, spiders and slugs – great food for birds. The cool, damp habitat may be secluded enough to offer daytime cover to a toad, or possibly frogs and newts from a nearby pond ■

appendix
2

Every garden is different and every gardener wants something slightly different from their own space. Some gardens only need a few modifications to make them more attractive to wildlife; others, particularly brand new gardens, can be designed specifically to include all the main wildlife habitats.

Designing a garden from scratch need not be as daunting as it at first seems. Look at as many other gardens as possible (particularly neighbouring ones which are the same shape and size) and make notes of features you would definitely want to include (use the checklist of wildlife features on page 13). It is a good idea to take a photograph of the garden, perhaps taken from an upstairs window to give an overview. This photograph can then be used as the basis of your plan – by laying over pieces of tracing paper, features can be drawn in to build up a picture of what the finished garden might look like.

GARDEN PLANS

A small, rectangular plot is quite simply adapted to the needs of wildlife.

KEY

❶ **Compost bin** provides organic material and a good hunting ground for insect-eating birds and toads.

❷ **Flowering meadow** supplies nectar for a wide range of butterflies.

❸ **Piles of logs** and leaves encourage beetles and other small insects – another food source for birds and small mammals like hedgehogs.

❹ **Shrub border** including native species like hazel and berry-bearing species like berberis and cotoneaster.

❺ **Pond** is vital for breeding frogs and newts and as a water supply for birds and mammals.

❻ **Marshy ground** adjoining the pond extends the plant species and offers cover to young amphibians.

❼ **Flower border** with nectar-rich and seed-bearing species will be visited by moths, bees and butterflies – as well as birds in the autumn.

❽ **Bird table** attracts birds to feed in the garden in winter and, hopefully, return to nest in spring.

❾ **Buddleia** bush has a place in every wildlife garden for the huge numbers of butterflies it attracts.

TRADITIONAL WILDLIFE GARDEN

138

A GARDEN FOR URBAN WILDLIFE

A wildlife garden can retain some formal elements, particularly in the areas closest to the house.

KEY

❶ Flower border crammed with nectar plants for bees and butterflies.

❷ Nesting box on a north- or east-facing wall for small birds.

❸ Climbers in pots, such as ivy and honeysuckle, attract a range of insects and may encourage birds to nest.

❹ Herbs in pots by the backdoor are handy for the kitchen and for passing bees and butterflies.

❺ Formal pond can be softened with poolside planting to offer cover to young frogs and toads.

❻ Compost bin is cleverly hidden behind shrubs, but still accessible to wildlife.

❼ Meadow is situated away from the house, giving an undisturbed natural area at the back of the garden.

❽ Trees can be incorporated in larger gardens as part of a 'woodland' belt.

❾ Mixed hedgerow of native species makes an excellent 'wildlife corridor' and an effective boundary between you and the neighbours.

USEFUL ADDRESSES

SPECIALIST NURSERIES AND PLANT SUPPLIERS

Many of the plants referred to in the book are available from garden centres and larger nurseries. However, some of the less widely grown native plants are only available through specialist suppliers.

John Chambers Wild Flower Seeds
15 Westleigh Road
Barton Seagrave
Kettering
Northants
NN15 5AJ

Wildflower seeds by mail order. Also selected range of bulbs, perennial plants and seedlings. Catalogue available.

Emorsgate Seeds
Terrington Court
Popes Lane
Terrington St Clement
Norfolk
PE34 4NT

Wildflower and grass seeds by mail order. Specialist knowledge of wildflower meadows. Catalogue available and advice given.

Jan Joyce
Lanhydrock Cottage
Back Lane
Skerne
Driffield
Yorks

Wildflower and cottage garden plants, herbs and unusual perennials.

Kingsfield Tree Nursery
Broadenham Lane
Winsham
Chard
Somerset
TA20 4JF

Native trees and shrubs.

WILDLIFE GARDEN CENTRES

The London Wildlife Garden Centre
28 Marsden Road
Peckham
London SE15

Natural Surroundings
Centre for Wildlife Gardening & Conservation
Bayfield Estate
Holt
Norfolk
NR25 7JN

WILDLIFE ORGANISATIONS

Bat Conservation Trust
c/o The Conservation Foundation
1 Kensington Gore
London SW7 2AR

Information, newsletters, local bat groups.

USEFUL ADDRESSES

British Butterfly Conservation Society
Tudor House
Quorn
Loughborough
Leicestershire

Annual species counts and information.

British Dragonfly Society
c/o 1 Haydn Avenue
Purley
Surrey
CR8 4AG

Journals, fact sheets, field trips, and meetings
for members.

British Trust for Ornithology
The Nunnery
Thetford
Norfolk
IP24 2PU

Annual species counts and information.

Countryside Commission for Wales
Plas Penrhos
Ffordd
Penrhos
Bangor
Gwynedd
LL57 24Q

Responsible for nature conservation and promo-
tion in Wales. (SNCO)

English Nature
Northminster House
Peterborough
PR1 1UA

Statutory adviser to the government on nature
conservation in England. A catalogue of their
publications and leaflets is available from Dept
ENA at the above address. (SNCO)

Royal Society for Nature Conservation
The Green
Witham Park
Waterside South
Lincoln
LN5 7JR

Information on county wildlife trusts and local
natural history societies.

Royal Society for the Protection of Birds
The Lodge
Sandy
Bedfordshire
SG19 2DL

Advice on wildlife gardening for birds; nest
boxes and bird feeders by mail order; videos,
books, magazines.

Scottish Natural Heritage
12 Hope Terrace
Edinburgh
EH9 2AS
Scotland

Responsible for nature conservation and promo-
tion in Scotland. (SNCO)

FURTHER READING

The Illustrated Flora of Britain and Northern Europe Marjorie Blamey and Christopher Grey Wilson (Hodder & Stoughton 1989) – a beautifully detailed account of every native and naturalised plant you are likely to encounter.
How to Make a Wildlife Garden Chris Baines (Elm Tree Books 1985) – the original account of Chris Baines' Midland garden.
The Joy of Wildlife Gardening Geoffrey Smith (RSPB 1989) – a personal view of gardening for wildlife.
The Flowering of Britain Richard Mabey & Tony Evans (Pbk. Chatto & Windus 1989) – a fascinating cultural history of Britain's wild plants.
Trees and Woodland in the British Landscape Oliver Rackham (Dent 1990) – a classic work on the history of woods and the workings of trees.
The Living Garden Michael Chinery (Dorling Kindersley 1986) – a detailed natural history of garden creatures and their life cycles.

ACKNOWLEDGEMENTS

With warmest thanks to the following people who welcomed us into their gardens and made us tea:

Mr & Mrs Bryant, Chadwell St Mary, Essex
Mr & Mrs Caley, Shouldham Warren, Norfolk
Mrs Winifred David, Kingston upon Thames, Surrey
Mr & Mrs Robin Don, Elmham House Gardens, Elmham, Norfolk*
Lady Harrod, The Rectory, Holt, Norfolk**
Mr & Mrs P Hickman, Thames Ditton, Surrey*
Jan Joyce, Skerne, Yorkshire
Miss Joan McCagney, Driffield, Yorkshire
Donald MacIntyre, Terrington St Clements, Norfolk
Julian Marsham, Gayton Hall, Norfolk*
Mrs Jill Monk, Dell Farm, Aylsham, Norfolk*
Mr David Moore, Lancing, Sussex
Mrs Susan Robinson, Shoreham-by-Sea, Sussex
Jill Turner, Streetly, West Midlands
Mrs Liz Turton, Garton-on-the-Wolds, Yorkshire
Jenny Van der Hoek, Baveny Wood, Worcestershire
Christine Vick, Peckham, London

* The gardens marked are open to the public on certain days each year under the National Gardens Scheme. Full details are given in the annual 'Yellow Book' – *The Gardens of England & Wales*, obtainable from bookshops.

**The Old Rectory, Holt is open each year for the display of wild snowdrops. The opening is held in aid of the Norfolk Churches Trust and details may be obtained from The Lodge, Millgate, Aylsham, Norfolk NR11, 6HX.

Special thanks to Mandy Little and Sarah Widdicombe. Also to Colin Harper who gave advice on bird and bat box construction and to 'Rosie', without whom this book would have been written a lot quicker.

INDEX

Cruickshank

INDEX